LONDON'S OVERGROUND

LONDON'S
OVERGROUND

John Glover

Ian Allan
PUBLISHING

London's Overground
John Glover

First published 2012

ISBN 978 0 7110 3524 9

Published by Ian Allan Publishing

an imprint of Ian Allan Publishing Ltd, Hersham, Surrey KT12 4RG.
Printed in England by Ian Allan Printing Ltd, Hersham, Surrey KT12 4RG.

Code: 1202/B1

Visit the Ian Allan Publishing website at
www.ianallanpublishing.com
Distributed in the United States of America and Canada by BookMasters Distribution Services.

On half-title page: *Kensington Olympia sees No 378 015 in the east side platform, now restored again to a reasonable length, with a train for Clapham Junction on 12 April 2010. Services here on National Rail have been much expanded, to the extent that London Underground decided to withdraw most of their District Line services from Earl's Court.* John Glover

Opposite title page: *Services on the reinvigorated East London Railway recommenced on 27 April 2010 and DC-only 'Capitalstar' unit No 378152 is seen at New Cross Gate Platform 1 on the following day. This was when the initial service only was in operation, so the train is reversing. Trains did not operate south of here in service to West Croydon and Crystal Palace until May. The special board attached to the front reads, underneath the Overground roundel, 'First Passenger Train, April 2010'.* John Glover

CONTENTS

INTRODUCTION

Where to start? That was the biggest single problem from the author's point of view. London Overground is a new concept in passenger services for the capital, with all sorts of innovative ideas. But railways are overwhelmingly long-term creations, and so much depends on the activities of our predecessors. Inspired or sadly mistaken, their works live on. Once built, change on a major scale can be very difficult.

London in the 21st century is a rather different place from that of the great railway construction period of the mid-19th century. London Docks, then full of shipping, are now London Docklands and a large office complex. The shipping moved down river, then to the East Coast ports, but it still requires servicing by rail. The word 'suburb' was hardly needed in those days, and the huge call that suburban development would later make on railway operation was little recognised. Road congestion changed from being a minor nuisance to a major problem, which only belatedly was it appreciated that main-line rail services could help solve.

Over the course of the 20th century, the railway moved from being a profitable enterprise judged purely on commercial grounds to one that, with public support, could provide huge social benefits to the areas it served. However, to do that it had to be exploited imaginatively.

As this book will show, there have been many influences to determine what was constructed, with several attempts to come to terms with the effects of volume growth and to influence service provision. The traffics may be divided between those that affect London directly, from either within or outside its boundaries, and those that are just 'passing through'.

Passenger requirements are not the same as those of freight traffic. The former load and unload themselves, and the latter doesn't complain if it is held at signals for long periods – though the consignors and consignees might. Operationally, they have to be treated very differently.

The major concern here is railway passenger traffic, and how to make the best use of the facilities available, or those that could be made available with some relatively modest investment. It refers in the main to

Above: The delivery of the Class 378 units allowed the retirement (as far as TfL was concerned) of the dual-voltage Class 313s, dating from 1976. On 10 February 2010 at Kentish Town West No 313120 on the left is on a North London Line train to Richmond, while No 378014, also dual-voltage, is arriving on a service to Stratford. John Glover

Left: The 'Sprinter' Class 150s operated the Gospel Oak-Barking service for many years, and No 150123 is seen arriving at Walthamstow Queen's Road station with a service for Barking on 13 April 2010. The location is surrounded by housing, though it is not far from the centre of Walthamstow if one knows the way. John Glover

INTRODUCTION

Right: *The new bridge on the restored Broad Street line, which carries the East London Railway over the Regent's Canal, is most impressive and is seen here on 4 June 2010 with an unidentified DC-only 'Capitalstar' unit crossing it.* John Glover

Right: *Still with three cars only, unit No 378027 approaches Richmond on 15 April 2010 with a train from Stratford. The appearance of trains with pantographs in third or fourth rail territory still seems a little curious. The former Southern Railway signalbox is behind the train.* John Glover

the national railway system, but only in a minor sense to the major routes. How well are some of the lesser known operations doing? What are their strengths and weaknesses? Can they be reconfigured and services boosted to make a greater impact and contribution to the movement needs of Greater London? None of this is to deny in any sense the contribution of London Underground over the years, but that organisation is largely peripheral in the present context.

This then is the story of the evolution, development and early operations of what is now known as London Overground, and how Transport for London hopes that it will transform the railway and its usefulness to communities in the areas that it serves. It is not in any sense an official publication. Part 1 describes the constituent railways of London's Overground; Part 2 describes how they were developed and the way in which this came about. The author also attempts to answer the question 'What next?'

John Glover
Worcester Park

1

The Constituents

CHAPTER 1: **THE THAMES TUNNEL**

Shoreditch-Whitechapel-Surrey Quays-New Cross/New Cross Gate

Right: This map of the East London Railway shows it and the local area as it was in 1953. Courtesy of The Railway Magazine

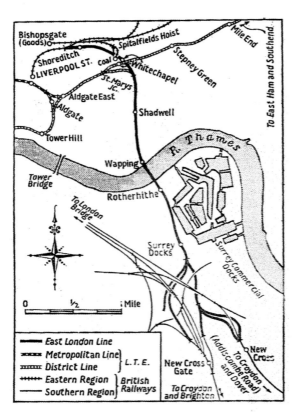

work was effected, a grand banquet for 50 people was held in the tunnel's western archway, the aim being to restore public confidence and to celebrate the resumption of tunnelling. Simultaneously, 120 tunnellers and bricklayers were provided with a less extravagant meal in the eastern archway. This was on 10 November 1827, but the Thames broke into the tunnel again on 12 January 1828, resulting in the loss of six lives and nearly that of Isambard Brunel, the son. The debris was cleared and work was suspended, but this time not restarted due to the exhaustion of funds. Some years later a pressure group of Fellows of the Royal Society was formed, and in December 1834 the first part of a government loan was received, arranged by the Duke of Wellington. This allowed the project to be restarted.

This time work was completed without major mishap and Queen Victoria opened the tunnel in January 1843, knighting Marc Brunel in the process. But there was no money left to construct the approach carriageways as intended, so the only way in and out was via the vertical shafts at both Wapping and Rotherhithe. This reduced its usefulness accordingly. Nevertheless, on the first day there were 50,000 visitors, and by the end of the fifteenth week a million people had each paid one (old) penny to walk through the tunnel.

East London Railway

Tunnels relying on pedestrian tolls for income are never going to make the substantial return on capital that was needed here, and the tunnel became more of a curiosity than a useful part of London's infrastructure. Fortunately, it had been built to dimensions such that it could accommodate the railway trains of the period. Thus its subsequent use was determined.

In 1865 the East London Railway Company was formed to acquire the tunnel and adapt it to railway use. This involved extending the tunnel north from Wapping to Shadwell, Whitechapel and Shoreditch, where a junction was made facing towards the Liverpool Street terminus of the Great Eastern Railway. Southwards from Rotherhithe the line was double track to Surrey Quays, then bifurcated at Canal Junction to New Cross (South Eastern Railway) and New Cross Gate (London, Brighton & South Coast Railway). The distance from Shoreditch to either New Cross or New Cross Gate was a little less than four miles, the latter branch being slightly shorter.

The Thames Tunnel runs from Wapping to Rotherhithe. It was completed on 25 March 1843, when it opened as a pedestrian thoroughfare. It was the first tunnel to be built successfully under a river anywhere in the world, and the engineer was Marc Brunel. He was later assisted by his son, Isambard Kingdom Brunel.

As long ago as February 1824 there had been an initial meeting in the City of London to promote the idea of a tunnel under the Thames, and considerable sums were raised by subscription. The intention was to build a tunnel that, with its spiral descending approach roads, would provide a means for carriages to cross the river. Thus the docks on the north side of the Thames would be linked with the industrial developments on the south. This would avoid the long diversion by the lowest Thames crossing at the time of London Bridge.

Work started in 1825, and was to be the first use of a tunnelling shield, driving under the river. Improved later by James Greathead, the tunnel boring machines in use today are its direct descendants.

Mishaps

This, however, was to be a very long-drawn-out period of construction, during which a total of ten lives were lost. In 1827 gravel dredging on the river bed caused the tunnel workings to be inundated by water. After repair

Opening

'An event that bid fair to be of great importance, but which has altogether failed to realise its promoters' hopes, was the opening on 10 April 1876 of the East

Left: *The East London Line platforms at Whitechapel are seen here in June 2003, looking towards Wapping and Rotherhithe. The platform on which the photographer is standing was used only when the Shoreditch service was in operation; at other times all trains terminated in and departed from Platform 5 on the far side.* John Glover

London Railway.' Thus wrote Dendy Marshall, historian of the Southern Railway. By this time it was complete throughout from New Cross Gate to Liverpool Street. The service was provided by the Brighton company, and in 1882 the line was leased in perpetuity to the Great Eastern, the London, Brighton & South Coast, the South Eastern, the London, Chatham & Dover, the Metropolitan and the (Metropolitan) District Railways. This latter resulted in the construction of St Mary's curve between Aldgate East and Shadwell (present names), opened in October 1884, when through steam services started. The spur to New Cross had been added in 1880.

The Metropolitan ran services from Hammersmith to New Cross. They were routed over the northern side of the Circle via Paddington and Aldgate East, then via the St Mary's curve on to the East London, terminating at New Cross (SECR). The District's equivalent ran via the southern side of the Circle to what is now New Cross Gate. These services ceased in 1905, after the Circle was electrified.

Other services such as those from the East London line to East Croydon and Peckham Rye were withdrawn on 1 June 1911, in view of the impending conversion of the East London to electric traction. They were not resumed, and that to Peckham Rye was the last passenger service to use the link between these lines.

Metropolitan electric trains started running on 31 March 1913, to New Cross and New Cross Gate only. Electrification was on the fourth rail DC system, with steam retained to operate freight services at night between the main-line railways. This was the last occasion on which a regular passenger train ran north of Shoreditch. The electric service included Hammersmith-New Cross trains over the northern part of the Circle as before. Such services ceased

finally in 1939, and the St Mary's curve then became used for stock movements (and specials) only.

The East London Railway undertaking was transferred to the Southern Railway by that company's Act of 1925, and in 1933 the newly formed London Passenger Transport Board acquired the former Metropolitan and Metropolitan District interests. The East London Railway Joint Committee (London & North Eastern Railway, London Passenger Transport Board and Southern Railway) was transferred to the British Transport Commission on 1 January 1948.

Post-war change

Thus what became the East London Line was formally vested in London Transport, which became wholly responsible for the infrastructure and passenger service provision. A variety of rolling stock was used over the years, and this is summarised in Table 1.1. The trains were usually hand-me-downs from the more heavily used subsurface lines of the Underground, though the appearance of 1938 tube stock for a few years in the 1970s was a surprise. Around half a dozen sets of trains was all that the line required. Rolling stock which was common to operations outside the areas covered in this book is not discussed generally. The line then entered a long, stable but unexciting period of its life. Operation was solely between Shoreditch and New Cross/New Cross Gate, which were the limits of fourth rail territory.

Up to and including the 1950s, through steam-hauled summer excursion services to the coast were operated through the East London Line tunnels, originated from such places as Enfield Town. These did, however, require reversal at Liverpool Street, after which they had to

Table 1.1: East London line rolling stock from 31 March 1913	
1913-37	Metropolitan Railway saloon stock of 1904-07
1937-39	District B stock of 1905
1939-53	District C, D and E stock of 1910 From November 1939, all ELL services were confined to that line only
1953-63	Metropolitan F stock 4-car
1963-64	District Q stock 4-car
1964-65	District CP stock 6-car
1965-71	District Q stock 4-car
1971-74	District CP stock 5-car
1974-77	1938 tube stock 4-car
1977-85	Metropolitan A stock 4-car
1985-87	District D stock 3-car
1987-2007	Metropolitan A stock 4-car

cross the entire formation from one side of the running lines to the other to reach Shoreditch. Quite apart from the locomotive requirements in terms of running round or providing a relief engine, such movements were not much liked by the operators for their effects on track capacity. To be fair, similar arrangements had to be made for freight traffic while that continued. The last British Railways through freight service ran in April 1966.

Severance

Following the cessation of traffic by these links, all physical connections with the main-line railways at Shoreditch, New Cross and New Cross Gate were severed by 1975.

All three terminal stations consisted of a single platform; this was a dedicated bay on the down side of the British Railways stations at both New Cross and New Cross Gate, while at Shoreditch the second platform became disused and had its track removed in 1969. Thus all services were operated exclusively by London Transport.

Patronage on the line north of Whitechapel to Shoreditch was relatively low, with service provision latterly confined to Monday to Friday peak periods plus Sunday mornings for the retail markets. Some use was made of Shoreditch as a commuter's economy package, since those originating from East London and who were prepared to walk from there to the City could use a Zone 2 ticket, which avoided paying the premium for travelling also in Zone 1.

When the Shoreditch service was not operating, East London trains were turned back at Whitechapel by using the crossovers south of the station and the northbound platform only.

The depot for electric trains was situated on the approach to New Cross station, with a total of six roads. A staff platform was provided on the running line. This was essentially a stabling point, and arrangements had to be made for trains to return periodically to a main depot, latterly Neasden for the London Underground A stock, which was the last to be used while the East London was thus operated. Latterly, these had to be selected from the 'double-ended' fleet, which could be used as single four-car units, as opposed to those for which one of the cabs was not modified and hence could be used only in the centre of eight-car sets.

The A stock and its predecessors used the St Mary's curve for access, the dimensions of which were so tight

Left: *The cramped conditions at Wapping, with the narrow platforms and single staircase access to each, are only too painfully obvious in this 1978 view of an A60 train emerging from the Brunel tunnel under the Thames. To be fair to the Brunels, the use of the Thames Tunnel for a railway was never envisaged during their lifetimes. The train is bound for Whitechapel.* John Glover

that only one train was allowed on the double-track formation at any one time. No trains in ordinary passenger service were routed this way. Another reason for this was that they would also miss calling at Whitechapel.

The East London line was converted to One Person Operation (OPO) on 13 May 1985. At that time the service was being provided by three-car sets of District D stock, which had been built with future OPO in mind.

Service provision

Between 20 November 1939, when all through passenger services on the East London line were withdrawn, and 22 December 2007, when London Underground operations finally ceased, the number of shuttle trains needed to run the peak service fluctuated between four and six. This reflected the changing commercial fortunes of the line and the extent to which services were projected to Shoreditch.

Off-peak, the minimum number of trains was two (in 1982) and, bearing in mind the need for services to be split equally south of Surrey Quays to reach the

destinations of both New Cross and New Cross Gate, this meant a very modest service of a train every 30 minutes to each. There were also capacity differences over the years in the sense that trains could be made up to a maximum of six cars (CO/CP stock) or as few as three cars (D stock). Typical point-to-point running times in 1990, before the opening of Canada Water, are shown in Table 1.2.

A round trip time to Shoreditch of about 30 minutes was achievable for each set of stock, including turnround times at each end; thus the 07:37 from New Cross Gate arrived at Shoreditch at 07:49. Use of a stepping-back Train Operator allowed departure at 07:51 to New Cross, arriving at 08:03. This train would form the 08:06½ departure from New Cross, with the same Train Operator. ('Stepping back' has the Train Operator of an incoming train at a terminus relieved by a Train Operator already on the platform, at what becomes the leading cab end. This does away with the time taken to walk the length of the train to reach the far cab against the flow of passengers. The first Train Operator then takes out the next incoming train, and so on.)

Modernisation

On 19 August 1999 the eight stations on the East London Line were supplemented by the wholly below-ground Canada Water station. As it was built for the A stock then providing the service, platforms were of four car length only. The station was opened principally for Jubilee Line interchange, but there is also a bus station at street level.

This station had the remarkable achievement of being built new between two stations (Rotherhithe and Surrey Quays) that were less than a kilometre apart anyway. The distance from Canada Water to Rotherhithe is a mere 340 metres. It is true that Wapping to Rotherhithe is only 530 metres, but the alternative of walking is not available as the Thames

Table 1.2: Running times, East London Line, 1990		
	Minutes	
New Cross and Surrey Quays	3.5	
New Cross Gate and Surrey Quays	3	
Surrey Quays and Rotherhithe	2	}
Rotherhithe and Wapping	1.5	} 7
Wapping and Shadwell	1.5	}
Shadwell and Whitechapel	2	}
Whitechapel and Shoreditch	1.5	

Above: *This is Surrey Quays station on 16 June 2003 with a southbound A stock train approaching. The bridge supports between the two running lines are a principal feature of this station at platform level and are a reminder of how rare a skewed bridge across the tracks is.* John Glover

lies in between. Inter-station distances in miles and chains are shown in Appendix B.

Surrey Quays received a new surface station in 1983, but unfortunately that at Shadwell (also 1983) was built rather further away than its predecessor from what was later to become the entrance to its Docklands Light Railway counterpart. Apart from routine engineering closures, there was a lengthy three-year period (24 March 1995-25 March 1998) when the entire line was closed for the upgrading, as it seemed at the time, of just about every facility – work that was supposed to have taken only seven months. This cost £110 million, of which £37 million was spent on strengthening the Thames Tunnel; slab track was also installed here.

The work was started only after a row with English Heritage had been settled. On the last day of operation before the closure, a spot Grade II listing of the tunnel by English Heritage meant that no works could be carried out without planning permission. Concerned about damage to the historic infrastructure, English Heritage wanted to see £400 million spent on a new rail tunnel, with the original returned to pedestrian use. Perhaps needless to say, English Heritage did not offer any funding. Agreement was reached in October 1995 and four tunnel arches at the Rotherhithe end, which were not actually under the river, remained unmodified.

Other work undertaken included resignalling, lift renewal, escalator installation, new lighting and the general refurbishment of the stations. An extensive network of bus replacement services was operated in the interim.

End of an era

In early preparations for the conversion of the line to a heavy rail system, to be described later, Shoreditch station was closed permanently on 9 June 2006. This site was not to be reused, since the replacement Shoreditch High Street station is on a different alignment at a different level (and is in fare Zone 1). Closure did, however, enable preliminary work on the new connection to the old Broad Street viaduct to get under way.

On 22 December 2007 the rest of London Underground's East London Line from Whitechapel to New Cross and New Cross Gate was closed for almost total reconstruction, albeit for a little less than three full years this time. The St Mary's curve connection was closed permanently and the track removed, while the sheds of the train stabling point at New Cross were demolished. For the next 2½ years East London passengers would again have to make do with buses, though this time the Jubilee Line was available for cross-river journeys.

Other railways

While the East London Line forms an important link in the London Overground network, many more railways are involved. Thus there are also lines of an orbital nature on the north, west and south sides of London, as well as a couple of radial lines that together make up the Overground network as a whole.

First, though, this book offers a general background to railway development around the capital.

Left: *This is the Southern Counties Touring Society's 'Metropolitan Railtour' from Stanmore to New Cross Gate on 1 October 1961 behind London Transport 0-4-4T locomotive No L44. The location is south of Surrey Docks station, when the freight link westwards, which forms part of the new line to Clapham Junction, was still in situ.* Ian Allan Library

Left: *The F stock with its distinctive elliptical cab windows was one of the types that took its turn on the East London and is seen here south of Surrey Quays. These trains were renowned for their ability to shift crowds quickly, though quite what use the facility might have had on this line is not known.* Author's collection

Building the railways

When the main-line railways of London are considered, they are nearly always thought of as radial routes, serving termini located more or less in the middle of the capital. And so they are, but this is only part of the story. Even in the early days, railways approaching from the north had to choose whether in passenger terms they were aiming at the City, or what became the West End. Or should they be looking at the wholesale markets to which they would be carrying goods traffic, the industrial eastern side of the capital, or the docks that in those days began not far beyond the boundaries of the City of London?

From west or east, the problem was equally difficult. Here, those market targets are reached successively, since central London is much wider east to west (from

Paddington to the City) than it is from north to south (from Euston to Charing Cross). Railways from the south had all the difficulties of those from the north, together with the expensive business of crossing the Thames.

Resolution was influenced by the findings of the Royal Commission on London Termini, which reported in 1846. The Commission ruled that the limits of encroachment by railways were to be Euston Road to the north, and the Thames to the south. And that, more or less, was what happened. Some marginal incursions across the Thames took place, notably to Charing Cross and Victoria, and, in the City, Cannon Street and Blackfriars. To say that these termini tended to be located on or near the traditional Circle Line of London Underground gives some idea of the extent of the central area of the capital, which was later to be served by the tube railways.

Other control over what the railways wanted to build was relatively weak, though each had to promote one or more Acts of Parliament to gain the necessary legal powers for its construction.

Walking to work

That was fine, up to a point, though times changed. In the 19th century suburban traffic was in its infancy, and the most common means of getting to work was to walk. But railways (and waterways) were the main movers of freight traffic to and from the capital, and access to what was then London Docks was a key requirement.

Thus modest incursion was permitted to serve the wholesale food markets. This produced what is now the core section of Thameslink between Farringdon on the Metropolitan and Blackfriars, for use by a number of the main-line companies. One way or another, they had physical connections with what are now known as the subsurface lines of London Underground. These were of course built to clearances approaching those of the main-line system, so full-size wagons could more or less be accommodated. The Metropolitan, it may be said, always considered itself a main-line railway anyway.

Thus a modest number of lines were constructed on the periphery (as it then was) of the capital, to forge some of the links that purely radial lines could not offer. Here the railway companies also came into contact with each other, physically in terms of having to bridge each other's lines at considerable expense or crossing them on the flat, with all the attendant problems of which company took precedence and the charges to be extracted from each other. They were also in competition for the traffic on offer, though this was a variable problem and dependent very much on location. Inter-company relationships would thus vary from active co-operation, through tolerating each other's presence, to outright hostility. The approach might also change over time.

This is not an aspect to be pursued in this book, but it is mentioned to remind the reader that treating the railways as a combined network that was generally open to all potential users was not found until the days of British Railways in the 1950s. Matters have since changed again with privatisation, but the national network itself still has a single owner in the form of Network Rail.

The following chapters now take the lines concerned in order, starting with the North London group.

Above: *This is Shadwell station at platform level on 28 April 2010 with No 378152 arriving from Dalston Junction through the brief daylight section. This area has been substantially cleaned up during the extended closure period and it is to be hoped that it will be kept that way.* John Glover

Left: *Wapping station was substantially rebuilt by London Transport in 1980. The building has changed little since, and the bus stop looks as though it would win any competition for that placed nearest a station entrance. The date is 28 April 2010.* John Glover

CHAPTER 2: **NORTH LONDON LINES**

Stratford-Dalston-Camden Road-Gospel Oak-Willesden Junction-Richmond

*Right The North London
Railway and its constituents
were linked to or crossed
a great number of other
railways as they threaded
their way around the north
side of the capital. This is
a chronological map, in
pre-1923 ownerships, of lines
west of Camden Road over
which the North London
maintained passenger
services. It refers to 1964,
so more recent developments
are of course omitted.
Courtesy of The Railway
Magazine*

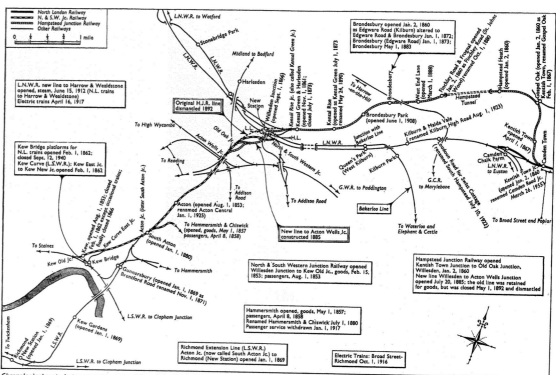

Chronological map, in pre-grouping ownerships, of the North & South Western Junction Railway, the
Hampstead Junction Railway, and other lines over which the North London maintains passenger services

The London & North Western Railway (LNWR)
approached London from the north-west rather than
the north. While its main line to Euston headed south
in a reasonably constant direction as far as Wembley
Central, it suddenly seemed to realise that continuing
on this trajectory would take it to Acton and Chiswick.
It thus made a decided turn to the east, followed by
another in the Willesden Junction area. After this,
it was heading not far short of north-east through
Kilburn, before resuming its former direction after the
Primrose Hill Tunnels and into its Euston terminus.

The line was thus quite remote from the London
Docks, and to reach them the most obvious method
was to build a line continuing due east at Primrose Hill.
And so it transpired, with the route from there running
right through to the long-closed Victoria Park and at
least the approaches to Stratford being remarkably
straight and thus direct. This quirk of railway geography
also accounts for the reason that the alternative route
from Willesden Junction via Gospel Oak to Camden
Road on the North London is so curvaceous.

The docks line was built by a second company with
the grand name of the East & West India Docks &
Birmingham Junction Railway. Incorporated in 1846,
the original line took it to the docks at Poplar. Further
Acts of Parliament saw junctions made with many
other railways over which it acquired running powers,

and the spur to Broad Street was opened as a City
terminus in 1865. This was reached via a triangular
junction at Dalston, and there was one intermediate
station at Shoreditch, the street-level buildings of
which are still extant. Another was added later, at
Haggerston. Three tracks were later increased to four
on what was almost all a viaduct structure but with
numerous bridges; this allowed services to run from
Broad Street to Poplar, as well as towards Willesden
and, in 1875, to the Great Northern via Canonbury.
Traffic increased rapidly, to the extent that there were
eventually nine terminal platforms at Broad Street.

Richmond was penetrated by running over the
tracks of the North & South Western Junction Railway
via Acton Central, but in 1908 what was now less
pretentiously called the North London Railway
became in effect a subsidiary of the LNWR, being
absorbed fully on 1 January 1922.

Besides its services to Bow and Poplar, the North
London also forged links with the Great Eastern
Railway, thus giving it access from the former Victoria
Park Junction to and via Stratford, and all that this
offered. That partnership was particularly rewarding
then in terms of the freight traffic accessed, which is
still intensifying in volumes today.

The Hampstead Junction Railway, incorporated
1853, built the route from Willesden Junction to

Camden Road via Gospel Oak. It was always worked by the LNWR, and was vested in it in 1867. The North & South Western Junction Railway was incorporated in 1851 and the Richmond services were worked by a Joint Committee of the LNWR, Midland and North London companies from 1871. At the Grouping in 1923, all were absorbed into the London Midland & Scottish Railway.

Electrification

The North London had extensive suburban services for which electrification became necessary because of ruinous competition from the electric tram. This produced passenger benefits in terms of cleaner trains and faster services. On 1 October 1916, Broad Street to Richmond via Hampstead Heath was electrified at fourth rail 630V DC, with a link from Kensal Rise to Willesden Junction Low Level. The section between Gunnersbury and Richmond had been electrified from as early as 1905, for the benefit of the District Railway. This had in effect determined the system of electrification to be used, in common with what was to become London Underground. The electrification scheme also included a projection over the important freight line from South Acton to Kew Bridge on the London & South Western Railway. Passenger trains here were withdrawn in 1940 and the link was subsequently de-electrified.

Timetable

The North London thereafter settled down. By 1938 it was operating a busy service to Broad Street. Arriving at the City station between 8.30 and 9.29am on weekdays was a total of ten trains – seven from Richmond and three from Kew Bridge. Not all trains called at all stations, Canonbury being the most common omission, then Caledonian Road & Barnsbury. Highbury & Islington, Camden Road and Kentish Town West were also sometimes omitted. The off-peak service was generally four trains an hour, with passengers to/from Kew Bridge getting a half-hourly service but needing to change at Acton Central. These totals exclude the services originating on the DC lines from Watford Junction.

By 1962 Broad Street arrivals from Richmond were down to a flat all-day service of four trains per hour (tph), reducing to three on Saturdays, which were by now devoid of any peaks. Sunday services started with two an hour, but increased to three and then four as the day wore on.

AC as well as DC

Although the former LNWR/LMS lines were electrified on the DC system in such a way as to be consistent both with each other and with London Underground, it became clear in the 1950s that electrification on the national scale was going to be at 25kV AC overhead. If other systems were self-contained or relied heavily on the Underground, that was perhaps a different matter, and the Watford DC line fell into both categories.

The Richmond to Broad Street line had much interaction with the freight railway and what might generically be called cross-London freight traffic, which was using it from (say) Willesden Junction through to Stratford. Importantly, this utilised the section east of

Left: This map shows the eastern end of the North London Railway through to Poplar, with developments to 1964. This demonstrates how it was once possible to access Fenchurch Street and the improvement wrought in terms of both directness and travel times by the opening of Broad Street in 1865. Courtesy of The Railway Magazine

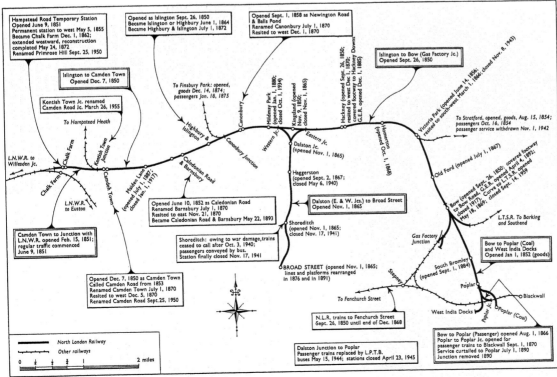

Chronological map, showing the North London line and associated railways

Above: A Class 313 unit in Network SouthEast livery crosses the eastbound bridge over the West Coast Main Line at Willesden Junction to reach the High Level island platform. In the background is Willesden High Level Junction signalbox, which then controlled the divergence of the West London Line and the North London continuation to Richmond. The train is bound for North Woolwich in this view of 23 March 1995. John Glover

Right: The North London was a railway of tank engines, which it built at its own workshops at Bow. This outside-cylinder 0-6-0T with wheels of 4ft 4in diameter for goods work was built under the direction of J. C. Park in 1879, as one of a class of thirty. They underwent several numberings and that shown here was built as No 15 and renumbered 2875 by the LNWR in 1922. It became No 7514 under the LMS, then 27514 in 1934. Finally British Railways decided on No 58855 in 1948. Some of these sturdy locomotives saw out their final years on the Cromford & High Peak Railway. Author's collection

Dalston Junction, which had been devoid of passenger services for many years. The cumulative effects of bombing and enforced station closures resulted in the remaining stations on the Poplar line closing on 15 November 1944. Then described officially as a temporary closure, passenger services to Poplar were never resumed. However, part of the route now forms a right of way for the Docklands Light Railway (DLR), and Devons Road, once the site of the North London locomotive depot, is now a DLR station.

The junction for Poplar at Dalston was removed in 1966 and the lines from Broad Street reduced to double track. Freight operations to Poplar Dock ended in 1983 and the approach tracks from Victoria Park Junction were subsequently lifted.

AC electrics

The short link from Primrose Hill to Camden Road was reached by 25kV AC electrification as part of the 1960s West Coast Main Line scheme in 1965. The purpose was to serve the then Freightliner terminal at Maiden Lane and had no implications for regular passenger operations. It did, however, enable British Railways London Midland Region to offer taster services for its new electric main line, by running the new AM10 (later Class 310) units on special excursions from Camden Road to Coventry. Many years later, electrification at 25kV AC was to become general on the North London Line.

Line potential

From Willesden Junction, where there are connections in many directions, there are two lines to Camden Road. From the High Level station, the northern route runs via a string of eight stations, including Gospel Oak. From the Low Level station the route reaches the same destination via Primrose Hill Tunnels and Primrose Hill station (closed in 1992). Eastwards from Camden Road there were four tracks; the passenger services used the pair on the south side, and in many cases these were the only ones equipped with platforms. Consequently, only these tracks were electrified on the DC system.

This four-track layout continued for just under three miles, past the stations of Caledonian Road & Barnsbury, Highbury & Islington and Canonbury, to the site of Dalston Junction, where the Broad Street line diverged. Along this route, a connection at Canonbury from the Great Northern at Finsbury Park allowed steam-hauled and later diesel-hauled passenger trains to reach Broad Street.

At Dalston, the four tracks were reduced to two for the continuation of the line towards Stratford. This was a freight-only route, but the approach to Stratford offered opportunities to access the Great Eastern main line (which itself provided a means of reaching the ports of Felixstowe and Harwich, or via Forest Gate Junction to Tilbury and the North Thames area generally). Other routes led to Temple Mills freight yard, and to the Stratford-North Woolwich branch.

New services

It was this last line, with its poor condition and operation by diesel units, that first attracted the attention of the Greater London Council (GLC). The Council had already been instrumental in providing an additional station on the North Woolwich branch at West Ham, which was opened in 1979. However, the potential availability of a line that passed through Hackney but carried no passengers was also an attractive proposition. This was the basis for the first round of investment, which had no electrification content but was a necessary precursor of what was to follow.

Clearly, the principal destination to be reached was Stratford, for which the infrastructure was already in place and available, and the choice then was to continue over the branch from Stratford Low Level to North Woolwich, which had itself seen better days. Services here were provided on a self-contained basis by British Railways Eastern Region, using diesel multiple-units (DMUs). The scheme embraced the following:

* Reopening of the line from Dalston to Stratford Low Level for passenger traffic. This took place on 14 May 1979, when an hourly passenger service was inaugurated.
* Provision of a DMU-operated service over the 11-mile route between North Woolwich and Camden Road. The latter was seen as the most suitable terminating point, where the trains could be

accommodated physically in the short term on the Primrose Hill spur, where they needed to reverse.
* New stations would also be needed on the intermediate section, and the four chosen locations were: Dalston Kingsland (1983), near to but not on the same alignment as Dalston Junction, which had platforms on the Broad Street spur only; Hackney Central (1980), near to but on a different line from Hackney Downs GE, which is further north; Homerton (1985); and Hackney Wick (1980). All these stations were to be sited on the section of the North London that had always been double track only, so there were implications for the freight traffic.

Above: Old-style manual platform indicators are seen here at Richmond in July 1985. Provided they are kept updated, few people can go wrong when looking at them, and they are not subject to the vagaries of bright sunlight effectively extinguishing them as can happen with their electronic replacements. But they do require staff presence and its costs. John Glover

DMUs

However, the Stratford-based Cravens Class 105 DMUs built about 1960 were not getting any younger. There were reliability problems, and the nominal half-hourly service frequency was irregular due to the need to interwork with other traffic. This included freight, as well as the basic service of three electric trains per hour between Richmond and Broad Street. The result was a proposal to electrify the line east of Dalston on the third rail system, which would add a further eight miles to the third rail network – and north of the Thames at that.

BR's 1982 estimate for this work was £10.3 million, later reduced to £7.1 million after making the inevitable economies. The GLC decided to fund this scheme on the basis of the social benefits it would bring to an area that was sadly in need of redevelopment. However, any suggestion that the existing service to Broad Street could continue unchanged was clearly not realistic. Consequently, the service provision proposal was to divert the three-trains-per-hour Richmond to Broad Street service to North Woolwich at all times, leaving Broad Street with a Monday-to-Friday peak-only service from Watford Junction. By 1984/85 this had been reduced to eight morning arrivals at Broad Street between 07:23 and 09:54, and six departures from 16:09 to 18:29, together with some contra-peak return workings.

Implementation

The most obvious work required the laying of the third rail eastwards from Dalston Junction right through to North Woolwich. Life-expired semaphore signalling was replaced with three-aspect colour lights, two signalboxes were closed, and signalling cables were immunised. The BR Automatic Warning System (AWS) was also installed. Traction power supplies were taken from the London Electricity Board at Maiden Lane and West Ham, with the dual supply intended to guard against total power loss.

The original proposal was to use the 1957-built Class 501 three-car units, described later. These had operated all the London area DC schemes of the London Midland Region since they were built. To an unexciting specification, which was limply called 'BR Standard Design', these three-car units were unusual for an Eastleigh production in having short 57-foot underframes. However, the possibility existed of using some two-car EPB Southern Region units of Class 416/3, themselves built on old Southern Railway underframes. Sixteen units were prepared for this duty, the 'conversion' consisting of fitting window bars, like the Class 501 units, because of the limited clearances in Hampstead Heath Tunnel.

Next phase

Yet this too was only a stopgap measure. The closure of Broad Street was now well and truly on the horizon and the then Transport Secretary, Nicholas Ridley, approved this in 1985. Railway usage was falling, and it was not perhaps altogether surprising that when the opportunity arose of selling the Broad Street site for development (Broadgate), the proceeds of which could be used for the total reconstruction of Liverpool Street, it was seized upon by the British Railways Board. Although Broad Street now hosted only the peak Watford services, these could not just be abandoned.

The only intermediate station affected by the closure was Dalston Junction, the platforms of which were on the branch only. Dalston Kingsland, about 250 yards away, was deemed to be a reasonable alternative.

Two alternatives were made available to passengers wanting the City. One was to change to the GN suburban services at Highbury & Islington, travelling underground thence to Moorgate. The other was to use a new service to Liverpool Street, for which new construction was necessary. This new west-to-south link acquired the name of the Graham Road curve, and was a single-track bi-directionally signalled link from Navarino Junction on the North London (a little to the east of the present Dalston Kingsland station) to the West Anglia line south of Hackney Downs. By this means, trains from the North London would be enabled to reach the Enfield Town line and hence Liverpool Street. As a terminus, Liverpool Street is adjacent to Broad Street, and a lot nearer than Moorgate, although too much should not be made of such distances – the difference was no more than a quarter of a mile.

The Graham Road curve was duly electrified at 25kV AC, but this was of course of no use to the DC-

Above: *The sinuous curve takes this train of tank wagons from Willesden round to Acton Wells on the North London Line, there to proceed either to the Great Western main line or on to the South Western via Feltham. It is 22 August 1979 and the locomotive is No 47008.* John Chapman

Left: *North London outside-cylindered 4-4-0T No 14, with a long train of four-wheeled coaches, is seen at an unknown location, but it seems likely that the train is on its way to Richmond. Locomotives of this wheel arrangement were the standard North London passenger engines, built to the designs of the company's locomotive superintendents, but none survived the 1923 Grouping for long.* Author's collection

only 2EPB sets. What was wanted for this was a dual AC/DC unit, for which the Great Northern Class 313 was an obvious contender – especially as there were some surplus to requirements. Consequently, the 25kV AC was extended from the Graham Road curve to Dalston Kingsland station, and this became the AC/DC changeover on such services, with pantographs being raised or lowered. This was in the same way as Drayton Park was used on the Great Northern & City line to Moorgate.

Broad Street closure

In order to allow the Broadgate developers to take over the site, a temporary platform was erected at Broad Street and brought into use on 30 September 1985. From that date a full complement of Class 313 units, purloined from the Great Northern services, was introduced to replace the remaining Class 501s.

The last train departed from Broad Street on Friday, 27 June 1986 from the far end of the one remaining platform, and the new service to Liverpool Street commenced the following Monday, 30 June. The service was provided by the Class 313 dual-voltage units and survived until 1992. Inevitably journey times to the City lengthened further, and it was not a success. Its withdrawal also saw the end of Primrose Hill station,

since this was the last passenger service to be routed that way.

Few mourned the passing of Broad Street, with the platforms perched as they were high above street level and reached by long sets of stairs. As a station it just grew sadder and more dilapidated over the last twenty years of its existence. Part of the roof was removed and platforms and tracks were abandoned successively. That it was once one of London's busiest stations was hard to believe.

Finally, the station site was completely cleared and the Broadgate Centre was officially inaugurated by Prime Minister Margaret Thatcher on 11 July 1986. The viaduct to Dalston Junction, however, remained in situ.

Freight goes AC

Little of the electrification work had any effect on freight traffic, but the need to traverse a few miles of the North London line in between substantial stretches of overhead-equipped railway was less than ideal. With the West Coast Main Line (WCML) electrified, in addition to the Great Eastern and the London, Tilbury & Southend lines, there was an opportunity to link the two systems. The beneficiaries were to be freight operations; any gains for passenger traffic would at best be incidental.

This meant electrifying the North London at 25kV AC, for which route there was little in the way of alternatives. The proposal was to complete the electrification between the WCML (Camden Road) and Stratford, and also into Temple Mills yard. This would mean the wiring of several other locations too. The objective was to improve locomotive utilisation and reduce time-wasting (and space-occupying) traction changes at Willesden. It would also result in 14 diesels of Classes 37 and 47 becoming surplus, albeit at the expense of four new Class 90 electric locomotives being needed.

About the only other possibility was the use of the Tottenham & Hampstead line (Gospel Oak-Barking), but that suffered from weak bridges and did not solve the question of what happened westwards from Gospel Oak towards Camden or Willesden. It was also of no use for traffic originating from the Great Eastern, notably but far from entirely from the Port of Felixstowe.

Small additional electrification projects at various locations were needed to allow trains to be electrically hauled through to their destination without the use of diesel power. In the immediate area another couple of miles of wiring gave access from the East Coast Main Line to Stratford and beyond. The line between Finsbury Park and Canonbury West Junction on the North London Line required the singling of the 545-yard Canonbury Tunnel to provide sufficient overhead clearances.

The proposal was sponsored by the BR Freight Sector, and was approved late in 1984 at a cost of £12.2 million. All work was completed by the end of 1987.

North London Incline

A further requirement for wiring was the steep North London Incline, between King's Cross Freight Terminal Junction and Camden Road. The distance is only 0m 49ch, but making it available meant that Class 313 units working on the North London could easily reach Hornsey depot and thus still be maintained there. This line was energised at 25kV AC on 11 November 1987.

Selective singling

Although the freight lines were double track between Camden Road and Dalston, it was decided in the interest of economy to reduce the centre section – the mile between Barnsbury and the approach to Dalston – to single track only, which reduced the work of increasing clearances on the dozen or so overbridges on this length of route. The four-track section was also cut back to two tracks for a quarter of a mile at Camden Road, the former north-side platforms being left devoid of track.

In retrospect, such capacity restrictions were decidedly unwise, but at the time this was a common approach to reducing both capital and maintenance costs. It can be defended on the grounds that it was

better than the only alternative then available, which was not to undertake the work at all. It also related to the extent to which the Freight Sector would be rewarded. It was the additional passenger trains that were at least as likely to benefit. Joining up AC electrification schemes also made other non-traffic moves rather easier, such as the ability to move electric multiple-units (EMUs) around more readily for maintenance purposes.

AC and DC

Thus the situation was created whereby what was now the Richmond-North Woolwich service was operated entirely by Class 313 dual-voltage EMUs with both overhead and third rail capability, although at this stage the services to Liverpool Street were the only ones requiring the AC function. Changeover took place during the station stop at Dalston Kingsland.

Above: Shoreditch LMS station building, part of the original North London operation. The station itself has been disused since the war, when it was closed following bomb damage. The platforms survived for many years, but were later cleared. The building, on the corner of Old Street, has found other uses and is seen on 28 April 2010. John Glover

CHAPTER 3: **LONDON EUSTON TO WATFORD JUNCTION**

Euston-Queen's Park-Harrow & Wealdstone-Watford Junction and branches

Right: This diagram shows how the DC electric lines from South Hampstead on the right were given nonconflicting routes to take them to Euston (top left) or Broad Street (bottom left). This required extensive tunnelling, so there is little to see from the passengers' point of view. It was, however, deemed to be of sufficient interest to feature (with full-colour cutaway drawings) in Eagle, the 1950s paper for boys. That artist was L. Ashwell Wood. This is a 1922 drawing. Courtesy of The Railway Magazine

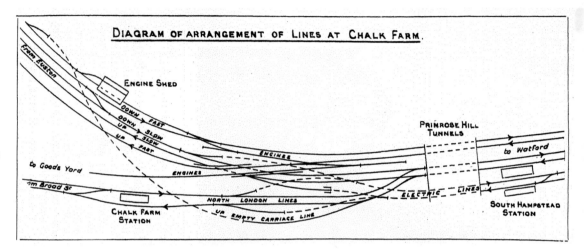

The London & Birmingham Railway opened to Euston in 1837, and this was the first main-line terminal in central London. True, the London & Greenwich opened to London Bridge a year earlier, but this was a line of modest local consequence only, and in no sense did it compare with the magnificence and breadth of vision to be found at Euston. Sadly, the Doric Arch and the Great Hall were victims of the 1960s rebuilding, but the enhanced Euston remains one of the great main-line termini.

Euston was built for the long-distance rail traffic of its day. The station was situated just to the north of the New Road, which itself was then being built. Known today as Euston Road (and Marylebone Road to the west and Pentonville Road/City Road to the east), it was to stretch from Paddington to the City. Places beyond, such as Wilsdon (now Willesden), were free-standing villages and no more.

As it turned out, the company had few aspirations for developing local passenger traffic, such as it might have been. With major business to be had in moving the raw materials and products of what were fast developing as the industrial heartlands of the Midlands and North, short-distance passenger traffic in modest volumes showed little potential. London was, of course, a major consumer of manufactured products, and the main line was progressively four-tracked in the latter part of the 19th century.

Suburban expansion

But this was still not enough capacity, and the suburban traffic needed attention. Thus was struck a partnership with the London Electric Railway for the Bakerloo Line. This line was extended from Paddington to

Queen's Park on 11 February 1915, and from there on would share tracks with newly instituted LNWR suburban trains from Euston.

New running tracks were constructed as far as Watford. At Euston, the suburban DC platforms were (and are) in the centre of the station, and these trains reach the east side of the main running lines through the junctions to the immediate south of the Primrose Hill Tunnels.

Primrose Hill

The complex series of grade-separated and mostly underground junctions enabled the six tracks approaching the Primrose Hill area from the north to be rearranged as they approached the terminus. From west to east, these are down fast, up fast, down slow, up slow, down DC, up DC. South of Primrose Hill Tunnels they are rearranged so that today they offer uninterrupted access to the low- and high-numbered main-line platforms at Euston, with the DC and slow line suburban platforms in the centre of the layout. Access, again uninterrupted, is also available between both the slow and DC lines and the North London at Camden Road. The whole is shown in the diagram on page 19.

As there is little to be seen on the surface, this major engineering feat is little appreciated for the benefit it confers on smooth traffic movements. It should perhaps also be remembered that in steam days the departure and arrival sides of Euston were strictly separated, that both light engine and empty coaching stock movements were often required, and that Camden, south of Primrose Hill, had a major goods function that created its own traffic.

Further north, the LNWR DC tracks use the outside faces of the two island platforms at Queen's Park, with the Bakerloo occupying the centre two. The double-track railway that follows remains on the eastern side of the main lines as far as Stonebridge Park, then crosses beneath them using a dive-under. From Wembley Central they remain on the west side of the WCML to their terminus at Watford Junction, following a diversion to the west to serve Watford High Street station. Between Euston and Watford Junction there are 19 stations in a length of 17¾ miles, and in 1938 the journey time was about 45 minutes.

It might be noted that Euston did not have to be the terminus for the electrics. In 1907 an alternative scheme had been proposed for a deep-level line that would run in a tube from South Hampstead with a station platform on a continuous loop under Euston itself. Thus the electric trains would merely continue, and not have to reverse direction. The idea was not pursued, although it raises interesting possibilities in the light of present circumstances. Underground access to Euston is relatively constricted (the Victoria Line and both branches of the Northern Line), and will become more so if the station is to host the London terminal of High Speed 2. The construction of HS2 itself will require the removal of the DC service while the works are carried out, maybe on a permanent basis.

Watford DC lines electrification

The London & North Western and North London Line electrification scheme was completed over a 13-year period from 1914 to 1927. This was a fourth rail 630V DC electrification with centre negative and outside positive conductor rails. The railway-owned power station was located at Stonebridge Park. In summary, events were as shown in Table 3.1. It should be noted that these are electrification and not opening dates.

The significance of the joint stock was that it was designed with a higher floor height to suit (as far as possible) both tube and main-line use. The 12 trains were divided in ownership between the LNWR (eight) and London Electric, later the Underground (four), reflecting this development as indeed being of a joint nature.

The Bakerloo's historian Mike Horne records that these were the only tube-type cars to have parcel racks. Perhaps the LNWR thought that they should look like the trains of a proper railway?

Above: As can be seen here on 17 November 1978, three-car trains of Class 501 stock departing from Euston fail to make full use of track capacity. The length of the main-line platforms in the foreground indicates how very much longer the trains might be. However, a fully loaded suburban train of 12 cars would be way beyond the capacity of many stations to cope, even assuming the demand was there on lines such as this.
John Glover

Table 3.1: Inauguration of Watford DC electrified services	
10 May 1915	Bakerloo trains extended from Queen's Park to Willesden Junction
16 April 1917	Bakerloo reaches Watford Junction and electric trains reach Watford Junction from Broad Street, via Hampstead Heath
1920	First jointly owned LNWR and Bakerloo stock is delivered, for Underground operation
10 July 1922	Full electric services inaugurated between both Euston and Broad Street and Watford, including electrification from Primrose Hill to Camden Road
23 October 1922	Croxley Green branch electrified
26 September 1927	Rickmansworth branch electrified

Above: A train of 1938 stock being used on the Bakerloo Line leaves the turnback siding at Harrow & Wealdstone in July 1984, shortly after Underground services had been restored there on 4 June. The train will proceed to Elephant & Castle. John Glover

New stations

To build a new line aimed at the suburban traffic was one thing; the other was to provide stations to access the new housing development that would follow. Eight completely new stations at sites not previously served were constructed on the DC lines in this period, and rather later in two cases. Thus the four stations of Harlesden, Stonebridge Park, North Wembley and Kenton all opened in 1912, as did Watford West and Croxley Green on a new branch. They were followed by Headstone Lane in 1913, Kensal Green in 1916, Carpenders Park in 1919 (though it was resited 231 yards south in 1952) and, rather later, South Kenton in 1933.

Mention should be made here of the substantial diversion between Bushey and Watford Junction. Here the DC lines head due west for a short time before turning back to the north. This deviation served three functions. The most important was to construct a station at Watford High Street, which as its name suggests was to serve the centre of Watford rather than outlying parts such as Watford Junction. The station built here reflected those hopes; it also enabled a triangular junction to be formed with the existing Rickmansworth branch and the new Croxley Green branch construction, and it provided access to the site for the car sheds that were built for the electric stock. Thus there was an ability to run directly from either branch to Euston as well as to Watford Junction.

After that there was virtually no change for many years. Automatic colour light signalling was installed on the DC lines in 1932, to improve line capacity. Willesden Junction High Level and Hampstead Heath both saw 1950s reconstruction to utilitarian-type designs, but essentially the situation was stable.

Third rail

The next significant change to the infrastructure came on 2 August 1970. This saw the use of the fourth rail system discontinued and replaced by the third rail as used on the Southern Region of British Railways. The replacement was not total, as the fourth rail had to be maintained in places where the infrastructure was used also by London Underground. As of today, this consists of the sections of the Bakerloo Line between Harrow & Wealdstone and Queen's Park, though it is in place as far as Kilburn High Road to enable recovery of any trains being misrouted. Occasional Bakerloo trains run out of service to Kilburn High Road and back to ensure that it remains operational. Fourth rail is also retained between Gunnersbury and Richmond for the District Line.

Bakerloo changes

London Underground wanted to build a new depot at Stonebridge Park as the only possible location for the separated Bakerloo Line operation following the

Above: *The symmetry of the station platform arrangements at South Kenton (1933) is there for all to see on 15 April 2010, and the general approach is similar to that adopted by the LMS company for the intermediate stations between Barking and Upminster.* John Glover

Left: *A Bakerloo train of 1938 stock leaves Queen's Park for the tunnel section to Elephant & Castle as another approaches on 22 July 1980. The shed to their left is used by London Underground to stable stock. On the left- and right-hand sides can be seen the tracks of the DC lines to Euston, complete with fourth rail to accommodate any mistakes by tube drivers accepting a wrong signal. The West Coast Main Line proper is on the extreme right.* John Glover

Above: *Stonebridge Park station sees Bakerloo 1972 stock arriving with a northbound service. Such trains can reverse either here (via the depot entrance behind the photographer) or at Harrow & Wealdstone. The style of the raised canopy on the southbound platform contrasts with the squareness of that on the northbound. John Glover*

Jubilee Line inauguration in 1979. However, the British Railways Board decided to make what in today's terms would be called high access charges. Perhaps needless to say, all tracks north of Queen's Park are part of the national network over which London Transport had running rights. However, there were no alternative depot locations for the Underground. Justified or not, such actions do not make for amicable relationships.

Bakerloo Line services were withdrawn between Stonebridge Park and Watford Junction on 24 September 1982. Watford was a very long way on an Underground train designed for short distances, and the traffic didn't warrant the double provision. Using the Croxley BR depot to house some Bakerloo trains overnight was also avoided. Service withdrawal did, however, result in huge protests.

Bakerloo trains were restored, but to Harrow & Wealdstone only, on 4 June 1984. There was thus a period of a little under two years when the stations of Wembley Central, North Wembley, South Kenton, Kenton and Harrow & Wealdstone had no Underground service. The service restoration was achieved on a quid pro quo basis. The North London Line services were having capacity problems, which would be expensive to rectify, while London Transport could offer the necessary capacity at small cost. A deal was done on the basis that each operator would bear its own operating costs, and that no additional charges would be made by BR for Underground operation to Harrow & Wealdstone.

Croxley depot was closed by British Rail with the withdrawal of the Class 501 fleet of trains, which had monopolised the service since they were built in 1957. They were replaced by the dual-voltage Class 313 units, although the ability to pick up from the overhead line was not used on any part of this network.

Croxley Green and Rickmansworth

These two branches were accessed from a junction south of Watford High Street. That to Rickmansworth Church Street opened in 1862, but was closed as early as 3 March 1952.

There were two intermediate stations on the single-line Croxley Green branch: Watford Stadium, opened in 1982, and Watford West. The first was not a public station, in that it was used only in connection with football matches.

The Croxley Green branch was later the subject of a proposal for a direct connection to be made to the Metropolitan line to Watford. The new line, double track throughout, will diverge from the old formation to a station at Ascot Road, using a new bridge to cross the intervening land containing the A412 road and the Grand Union Canal. It will join the Metropolitan east of the present Croxley station, and Watford (Metropolitan) station will be closed. A station at Watford General Hospital on a new site will replace the former Watford West. The scheme is championed by Hertfordshire County Council.

Croxley Green rail services were effectively withdrawn in 1996. The Secretary of State for Transport announced in December 2011 that the government was prepared to contribute £76.2m towards the £115.9m cost. Work is to start in mid-2014, with completion early 2016. 'An extra rolling stock unit will be required' (presumably a train), and a service of up to 7tph will be provided.

The relevance to London Overground is the effect that this might have on traffic levels via Harrow & Wealdstone and the use of the line and terminating capacity on the last stretch to Watford Junction. This will result in London Underground's Metropolitan line becoming a second operator over the northern end of the DC lines.

Conceivably, Chiltern Railways could also provide services by this new route.

Above: *One of the more unusual pieces of railway infrastructure to be found on the Watford DC lines is this railway overbridge and underbridge immediately in front of a tunnel entrance. This is the north end of the South Hampstead tunnels, where the ex-Great Central main line crosses the line out of Euston. The GC is also in tunnel on each side of the WCML. It may be added that all this can be seen from South Hampstead station platforms, in this case on 12 September 2009.* John Glover

Left: *Watford High Street station lies in a steep-sided cutting but has been well laid out as is desirable for a busy station in the town centre. No 313019 is seen leaving for Euston on 20 October 1998.* John Glover

CHAPTER 4: **TOTTENHAM AND HAMPSTEAD**

Gospel Oak-Barking

Right: *The Tottenham & Hampstead line has two electrified sections, neither of which does the local services any good. This westward view is of South Tottenham, with one of the stalwarts, two-car diesel unit No 117701, providing a Gospel Oak-Barking service in April 1997. The length of the overhead section is little more than the length of the platforms, and is provided to link the Enfield line (at Seven Sisters) to the Lea Valley. This single-track link starts in the middle of the platform; note the missing bit to allow vehicles taking that route to swing as they do so. The unevenness of the T&H route is emphasised by the dip needed to pass below the Enfield line in the distance.* John Glover

Winding its way through north-east London is the line that has in recent times been called Gospel Oak to Barking. Indeed, from a passenger viewpoint it starts today at a bay platform at Gospel Oak and uses successively the formations of the Tottenham & Hampstead Junction Railway (to South Tottenham, 1868), then the Tottenham & Forest Gate Railway (to Forest Gate Junction and Woodgrange Park, 1894) and the Eastern Counties/Blackwall thence (to Barking and beyond, 1854). The long-drawn-out construction period shows that it was far from being conceived as an entity, and ownership was likewise divided.

The original Tottenham & Hampstead latterly came under the joint control of the Midland and Great Eastern companies, the section to Forest Gate the Midland and what became the London, Tilbury & Southend Railway (LTSR), and the last section the LTSR proper. A triangular link at the western end to the Midland at Kentish Town was soon provided. With the links to the Great Eastern at South Tottenham, this gave the Midland access thence to Stratford and Fenchurch Street for passengers, and goods to the docks. Other destinations such as Chingford had services provided by the Great Eastern. Suburban traffic grew as homes were built, and was complemented by a very adequate rail service from the Midland Railway.

The opening of the link through to Barking gave the whole a new purpose, with Midland suburban services extended to Barking and the Tilbury company achieving access to the northern suburbs and St Pancras. The Midland was also able to reach the docks at Tilbury (for boat trains for passengers as well as freight), and

both companies were able to operate independently of the Great Eastern and North London undertakings. Excursion traffic to Southend was also possible.

The Midland acquired the London, Tilbury & Southend company on 1 January 1912, and the Tottenham & Forest Gate Railway Co (Midland) was absorbed into the LMS on 1 January 1923. The Tottenham & Hampstead Joint committee (GE&MR) was transferred to the LMS & LNER Joint Committee at the Grouping and to the British Transport Commission on nationalisation.

The route as a whole is known much more comfortably in railway shorthand as the T&H. It should be noted that this is a description of the railway and not of the passenger trains that run on it.

Service decline

The inter-war period saw peak-hour T&H trains to and from Moorgate via the Widened Lines, and a more or less half-hourly frequency otherwise. Later, the services were cut back, and diesel unit operations began in 1960; by 1962 these were operating from Kentish Town to Barking only, with negligible exceptions. Frequencies were by now much reduced, with two trains an hour in the peaks reduced to only one at other times on Mondays to Fridays. Saturdays retained a half-hourly service, and Sundays could best be described as mixed frequency.

The Kentish Town link was eventually closed on 5 January 1981 and the service was rerouted to terminate at a new bay platform at Gospel Oak, which was added to the north side of the eastbound platform at the North London Line station. While this gave cross-platform interchange between this pair of platforms, those whose journeys involved a westbound North London Line service had to contend with a long and wearisome walk to ground level and back again.

The T&H passenger service thus became an offshoot of the North London Line rather than the Midland, and the direct connection with London Underground's Northern Line at Kentish Town was also lost.

The service pattern changed little. By 2000 the frequency was half-hourly during the day, every day, but hourly in the evenings.

The railway

There are 12 stations on the T&H, and the off-peak journey time for the 12 miles is 36 minutes at a stately 20mph average speed.

The problem with the T&H was that it could easily be construed by the public as being not very relevant to their journey requirements. The station at Walthamstow Queen's Road is hardly at the centre of Walthamstow, and any connections with the Underground were seemingly more by chance than design. The Victoria Line station at Blackhorse Road opened in 1968, but the entrance was on the opposite side of the road from that of the T&H. It took until 1981 to resite the T&H platforms and operate the whole as one unit. For the most part, especially at the eastern end, the line was (and is) on viaduct and largely out of sight of the public. This meant long staircases to reach basic facilities on the platforms. Station staffing was cut back wherever possible, and the whole was operated as a basic railway.

Freight

There are, however, connections that enable the line to be used for freight traffic. Thus it is noticeably straightforward to access Tilbury and the North Thames area at Barking due to the flyovers constructed there in the late 1950s, and Stratford via South Tottenham as mentioned, with limited access to (but not from) the Great Northern at Harringay, to the Midland, and to Willesden via the North London at Gospel Oak. The connection at Gospel Oak was introduced as an emergency alternative route during the First World War, and was later lifted, only to be relaid in 1940 together with that at Harringay.

Traffic in more recent times has been limited by the condition and weight-carrying capabilities of bridges, and also by restricted clearances for large containers. The line is not electrified other than the short portion through South Tottenham station, which permits the operation of electric passenger services between the Enfield Town line and Stratford. Also electrified is the portion between Forest Gate Junction and Barking (but not the branch platform), which is used by electrically hauled freights to and from the Great Eastern network.

Above: *The former site of Blackhorse Road station (it is now on the other side of this road overbridge vantage point) shows little of its earlier use. The wall on the left marks the route of the access pathway. The date is 7 November 1998 and No 117706 departs with a Barking service.* John Glover

Below: *Class 127 DMBS cars, Nos M51640/10, are providing the service to Barking as it enters Leyton Midland Road station on 18 February 1984, having worked from Cricklewood depot. The T&H line is ideal for a rooftop-level view of East London, but less satisfactory from the point of view of the number of stairs that need to be climbed. Shorter-distance travel by bus needs much less effort.* Mick Roberts

CHAPTER 5: **WEST LONDON AND WEST LONDON EXTENSION**

Willesden Junction-Clapham Junction

Above: The use of steam traction on the occasional Clapham Junction-Kensington Olympia shuttle service required the locomotive to run round at each terminus. Here, Standard Class 3 2-6-2T No 82019 is making this move at Kensington Olympia on 26 April 1967. The end of all steam working on the Southern Region was only three months away. John Glover

The Birmingham, Bristol & Thames Junction Railway was incorporated in 1836, but its name was changed to the West London Railway in 1840. It originally started life in 1844 as no more than a branch from what is now Harlesden to the Warwick Basin on the Kensington Canal. In so doing, the railway passed under the Paddington Canal and made a flat crossing of the Great Western main line. The Kensington Canal was linked to the Thames at Chelsea.

The line was not a success. There was a minor dalliance with the atmospheric system of traction, but nothing came of it. It was subsequently leased to the London & Birmingham and Great Western railways, and eventually totally reconstructed to double-track status with a grade-separated crossing of the Great Western as well as a running connection. It did, however, have considerable potential.

Further work saw the creation of the West London Extension Railway (WLER), in which the railway companies south of the Thames also became partners.

This saw the canal filled in and largely built over by the railway, and also required the construction of a substantial bridge, Chelsea Bridge, to cross the Thames.

A highly complex series of burrowing junctions was built on the approach to the South Western and Brighton main lines as the WLER reached Clapham Junction. The result was Latchmere No 2, Latchmere No 1 and Latchmere No 3 Junctions, in that order. These allowed trains from the WLER to run, without reversal and with minimal conflict:

* down the LSWR line to Richmond
* down the Brighton main line to Croydon
* up the LSWR main line to Waterloo
* up the Brighton line to Victoria
* up the Chatham line to Victoria
* down the Chatham main line to Brixton

A further connection was provided by the Chatham company from the Richmond lines of the LSWR to its own main line and Brixton. It might be added that the South Western main line could be reached from Willesden Junction via Kew Bridge, Feltham and Addlestone. It was these connections, at the north and south ends of the West London Line, which a century and a half later were to provide a means of creating the London orbital services of London Overground.

Willesden Junction to Earls Court

The potential of the WLR/WLER could now really be exploited. Electric services were inaugurated over the West London line and its extension between Willesden Junction and Earls Court on 1 May 1914; the connection to the Underground was via the present route used by the District Line. The work included the connection from Latimer Road on the Hammersmith & City route of the Underground to Kensington Olympia (all present-day names). This was the first stage of the London & North Western electrification to be completed; subsequent delays were occasioned by the 1914-18 Great War.

The power station at Stonebridge Park was yet to be completed, and meanwhile power was obtained from substations on the Great Western's Hammersmith & City and the District Railway. On this fourth rail 630V DC system the conductor rails were supported on porcelain insulators attached to the sleepers by malleable iron clips, special anchor insulators being provided at intervals to prevent rail creep. Each rail joint was bonded.

These services were withdrawn on 19 October 1940 north of Kensington Olympia following bomb damage, and were never restored in that form.

Traffic

By 1930, Kensington Addison Road station (Kensington Olympia from 1946) had two through tracks flanked by two exceptionally long platform tracks, plus two bay platforms at each end on its eastern side. There were also goods sidings to the north. In 1958 a siding on the west side at the south end was converted into the District Line terminating bay, which led eventually to the total operational separation of the Underground tracks from the main line.

In earlier days a large variety of essentially local train services operated over the West London route, but freight was far more in evidence. This was, after all, a main railway artery, linking the main lines from the industrial North of England across London to the Channel ports. Thus passenger traffic on this essentially orbital route dwindled, having been seen off by the electric trams, the Underground and the buses, but also by the restrictions imposed by the Second World War.

The West London Railway Co (LMS & GWR Joint Committee) and West London Extension Railway Co (GWR, LMS and SR) were both transferred to the British Transport Commission on 1 January 1948.

Post-war

In the post-war years, the only passenger services on British Railways were those that ran between Clapham Junction and Kensington Olympia for Post Office Savings Bank employees. These operated twice in the morning and twice in the afternoon on Mondays to Fridays only. They were originally barred to public use, but this was later relaxed. Nevertheless, passengers were carried only from Clapham Junction in the mornings, and from Kensington Olympia in the

Below: The West London Line and its extension forms an important north-south link, notably for freight but increasingly nowadays for passenger traffic. This map shows the situation as it was in 1969 with one intermediate station only. Ian Allan Library

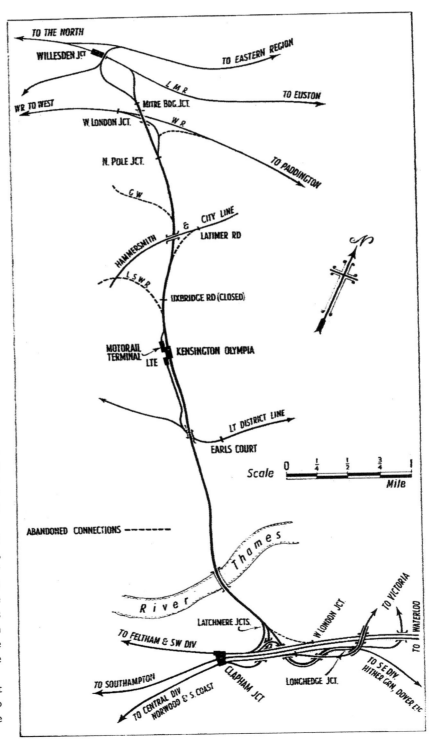

Above: A variety of rolling stock was used for the Clapham Junction to Kensington Olympia service over the years, and for a time this was the province of a Class 33 and a couple of Second Class coaches. Here No 33042 is seen from the former southbound (and little-used) platform, having run round its train and ready to return. Later a Class 33 plus 4TC push-pull unit was substituted. John Glover

afternoons. This was a fabulously expensive service to run, originally steam but latterly operated by a Hampshire diesel unit brought up from Eastleigh in the early morning, making its two return trips and laying over during the day. It then performed the evening task, and returned light to Eastleigh. Thus for a long day's work it covered a mere 170 miles, of which only about 15 were revenue-earning.

Much later this service was extended to Willesden Junction High Level, and was operated throughout the day. An additional station was constructed at West Brompton and this opened on 30 May 1999. This became, in effect, an extension of the adjacent District Line station with which it shared access to the street.

The West London Line was also used for summer holiday traffic from the Midlands and beyond to the South Coast. Motorail trains began in 1965, for which a covered loading bay was built on the west side of the station. These were designed to take passengers and their cars direct to holiday destinations in, for instance, Cornwall. It was again mostly summer traffic.

Use was also made of Kensington Olympia to substitute for Paddington or Euston during major engineering works in the 1960s and 1970s.

Later, British Railways decided that Kensington Olympia would make a good, almost pseudo, InterCity station. The idea was to free London terminals of some traffic by running through trains across London to Southern destinations, particularly Brighton but also to

Kent. This illustrates both the physical railway connections with which the West London Line abounds, and the potential of Kensington Olympia as an accessible location.

Economy measures then took place. The up (southbound) platform loop was removed, and a simple very short platform was built on what became the only up line. It might be mentioned that the effect on traffic was less dramatic than this suggests, as it coincided with the 1980 Victoria resignalling. Both through lines and the down-side platform loop were made reversible, and this allowed InterCity trains going south to cross the formation via the crossovers provided and use the platform on the down loop. This did not exactly help with any line occupation problems, and the move proved to be extremely short-sighted, for the new platform on the up side was suitable for two-car operation only, which was not going to be sufficient.

Revitalisation

Electrification (strictly re-electrification) from Clapham Junction to Willesden Junction, long talked about, was to become a reality, and was a side product of the construction of the international Eurostar train depot at North Pole. But what system should be used – third rail DC for compatibility with the Southern, or 25kV AC as the standard system in Britain? To add to

the complications, the lines through Willesden Junction High Level and thence to Broad Street (and also Richmond) were now third rail DC, and the east-west line was subsequently to be converted to 25kV AC.

Eurostars were built to run on both third rail DC for the journey from the Channel Tunnel to Waterloo over classic tracks, and various overhead systems in the Channel Tunnel, France and Belgium. However, for depot conditions overhead is much preferable to third rail, given the importance of staff safety in an area where there are many more people working at ground level. Thus, as the Eurostars were equipped with 25kV AC capability, there was good reason to use this in the depot area.

This therefore required there to be a changeover point in electrification systems. In the end that point was chosen as being on the West London Line between the north side of the A40(M) Westway overbridge and a point slightly to the north of North Pole Junction. The changeover is effected by the driver, and is made between those points, which are a little over half a mile apart.

Electrification north from Mitre Bridge Junction would have allowed Eurostar North of London and Overnight Sleepers to Europe to operate, but neither of these ever materialised. Local services were, however, able to use the Class 313s from the Great Northern to reach Willesden Junction High Level station and also permitted the introduction of Gatwick/Brighton to Watford/Rugby services by what is nowadays Southern, using former Thameslink Class 319s. Such trains cannot call at Willesden Junction even if it was so desired, since the main-line platforms there were closed in 1962 and physically removed.

Line capacity

Movements of Eurostars constituted a considerable burden on West London Line occupation, but the situation turned out to be only temporary. They concerned Waterloo initially, but to reach the High Speed 1 line in the Stratford area would have first meant reversing somewhere south of the North Pole Junction area before traversing the North London line to reach Stratford and HS1. Fortunately, this situation never arose, since Eurostar built a new depot at Temple Mills near Stratford. The North Pole facility was abandoned when the Eurostar services were removed to London St Pancras International in 2007.

So far, so good, but the West London Line is the primary freight artery on the west side of London. Indeed, it is the furthest point east at which freight trains can cross the Thames, with the Thameslink route at Blackfriars unsuitable due to severe gradients and tight curves. While HS1 provides for freight between the Channel Tunnel and Dagenham, where it connects to the Ripple Lane yard, at the time of writing it has had no regular use.

Thus freight is an important element of West London Line traffic, both in terms of train paths used and train paths that are contracted to freight operators as being available but which may in reality see little or no traffic. These have been a long-term problem for train planners.

Above: *Some of the locomotives ordered as part of the Kent Coast electrification were later converted to electro-diesel operation, though they didn't last long in that guise. Class 74 No E6105 heads south through the future West Brompton station site with a goods on 14 August 1973. A train of CO/CP stock can just be seen in the nearby London Underground station.* J. Scrace

Above: The terminus of London Overground at Clapham Junction looks as if it will be both ends of Platform 2, seen here with No 378022 on 4 June 2010. Fortunately it is long enough to take two four-car trains, even allowing for the need for a crossover in the middle of the platform. John Glover

Right: This is the new West London Line station at Imperial Wharf at platform level on 12 April 2010, with a northbound train provided by No 378006. The traffic growth here and at the other new station of Shepherds Bush has been substantial, to the effect that crowding is reported as preventing some passengers from boarding. John Glover

CHAPTER 6: **SOUTH LONDON LINE**

Victoria-London Bridge and Surrey Quays-Clapham Junction

This line was a joint creation of the London, Chatham & Dover Railway and the London, Brighton & South Coast Railway, by which they both achieved their respective goals. Today the northern pair of lines on the four-track stretch between Wandsworth Road and Peckham Rye are the Chatham lines and used by Southeastern; the southern pair, which form the South London, are the Atlantic lines, used by the Brighton. A complication is the diverging junction at Brixton, where the branch from the Chatham lines route has to pass under the Atlantic lines; the latter thus have to pass over the top, and the implications of this will be discussed later.

The Brighton chose an AC overhead system for electrification, and this was completed on the first line from Victoria to London Bridge on 1 December 1909. This was a response to the introduction of electric trams on the roads, which were eating seriously into railway traffics in the Edwardian era. Similar considerations prompted urban railway electrification in several other British cities.

This was a high-tension single-phase 6,600V AC system, with overhead conductors. Power was obtained from the London Electricity Supply Corporation at Deptford. Motor and trailer cars were provided for two- or three-car sets of compartment stock. Electric working was inaugurated on the South London Line on 1 December 1909, followed by further sections until 1925. By this time electrification had reached as far as Cheam.

The Brighton became part of the Southern Railway on 1 January 1923, but according to Charles Klapper's biography of Sir Herbert Walker, the new management did not give much attention to overhead power supply. They were certainly not interested in the Brighton company's system. Acceleration was poor, construction was slow and German-made equipment was involved, tricky in those days. Conversion of the Brighton's AC system to third rail was completed in September 1929.

The route

The traditional South London Line runs from London Bridge to Victoria, less than three miles apart in a direct line. However, the sinuous nature of the South London means that the end-to-end distance is almost nine miles. Trains call at seven intermediate stations, and take around 25 minutes to complete the journey; they run at half-hourly intervals and there is no peak supplementation. The stations at Peckham Rye, Denmark Hill and Battersea Park all have other services and thus connectional opportunities, but are otherwise unrelated to the South London Line proper. The line is sometimes known as the Inner South London Line, to distinguish it

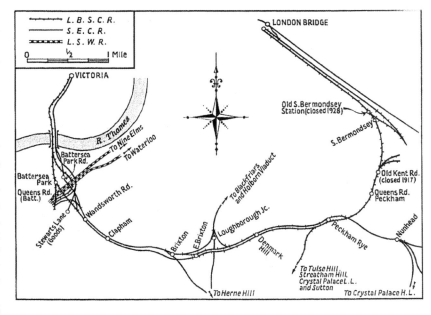

from the Outer South London Line from London Bridge to Victoria via Gipsy Hill and Balham.

This railway is not aimed at end-to-end travellers, but more at carrying the intermediate traffic, which in later British Rail days was certainly limited. Passenger carryings at the free-standing stations at the western end of the route, Clapham High Street and Wandsworth Road, were in the dire category, with well under 50 passengers a day joining trains at either of them in 1991. As is commonplace in the inner areas of South London, most of the route is on viaduct, and stations are thus rather less visible to the potential passenger than they might be.

One of the results frequently seen was termination of the western end of the service at Battersea Park, where passengers to and from Victoria had to change platforms via the subway. This had the operational benefit of offering a more reliable service using two train sets only, as the running times for the full journey allowed very little leeway for late running. It was not, however, popular with passengers.

At least as important was the freeing up of line capacity on the Brighton slow lines out of Victoria, which could then be used for other purposes. Trains that provide adequate capacity with two cars only for the route served do not count highly in the pecking order if the aim is to shift as many people as possible within the infrastructure resources available.

Economies

There have been economies. As long ago as 1959 the Sunday service was cut down to operate between

Above: *The circular nature of the South London Line is immediately apparent in this 1953 map, showing pre-Grouping ownerships. Today Denmark Hill and Peckham Rye are the only stations to have platforms on both of the pair of parallel lines. The junction reinstated for the connection to Surrey Quays is shown at the site of the closed Old Kent Road station. Courtesy of The Railway Magazine*

Battersea Park and Peckham Rye only, which meant that one train could operate the whole service. As a letter from the Southern Region's District Traffic Superintendent said, 'The costs of operating this route on Sundays have considerably exceeded the receipts for some time. It was considered that this arrangement would be better than withdrawing the service altogether.' This had resulted in broken connections, and the complainant is worth quoting:

'Until recent amendments, connections at Denmark Hill between South London and Catford Loop trains have been reasonably good. Now the down Catford

Loop train will depart one minute before the South London train arrives at Denmark Hill so that the unfortunate passenger now has a wait of 29 minutes. In the opposite direction the wait is not so bad, but bad enough at 17 minutes.' (In the event, throughout Sunday services were later restored.)

This episode illustrates one of the perils of an even-interval service, in that if the connection is bad on one occasion, it is always going to be bad, every time. (Conversely, it can also be very good.) The other problem is the degree of interaction between services, especially in as complex an area as the South Central network. Thus retimings to correct a problem may well have unfortunate consequences elsewhere, and so on. The only real solution to this is to run a more frequent service, but if the traffic isn't there the justification is equally elusive.

Victoria

All trains in more recent times have run to and from Victoria. Once the haunts of Southern EPB units and similar, most are now formed of a single Class 456 two-car set with about 150 seats. Occasionally these are made up to four cars.

Changes have been few, with perhaps the last of note being the closure of East Brixton station. Because of falling demand and the poor state of the buildings, Ministerial consent was given to its closure from 5 January 1976. Today this accounts for the higher than usual two-mile gap between Clapham High Street and Denmark Hill stations, but has allowed the running times to be reduced slightly.

The South London is an unassuming railway that has operated with only minor changes for very many years, and which might have been expected to continue thus. Change, though, would have come with the present rebuilding of London Bridge station.

Above: The twin stations
at Peckham Rye are linked
internally. This side serves
the lines on which Southern
Railway No 456024 is
departing with a service from
Victoria to London Bridge.
Southeastern services use
the other pair of platforms
to the left. The date is
15 April 2010. John Glover

Left: The delightful station
building at Denmark Hill is
nowadays mostly turned over
to pub premises, although
a full four platforms remain
below. But only the intrepid
will be able to find their
way in as signing is woefully
inadequate. The station is
managed by Southeastern
and was photographed on
15 April 2010. John Glover

CHAPTER 7: WEST CROYDON AND CRYSTAL PALACE

New Cross Gate-Crystal Palace/West Croydon

Right: The Brighton main line from London Bridge has four tracks, with platforms (mostly) on the slow lines only. Here at Brockley No 378144 is undertaking a crew training run towards West Croydon on 12 April 2010; a Southern Class 455 unit is forming an up service which is in passenger use. John Glover

From the Brighton side of the station at London Bridge, what is now a four-track railway extends to the Windmill Bridge Junction area outside Croydon. Here, the line to West Croydon diverges, and the main line from London Bridge amalgamates with the similarly four-tracked line from Victoria. The four-tracking continues, in effect, for 31 miles from London Bridge to Balcombe Tunnel Junction, which is well south of Three Bridges.

That from London Bridge is the earlier main line, by some margin. It was opened by the London & Croydon Railway in 1839 to take it to the present West Croydon. The line was built largely on the formation of the Croydon Canal, which the company acquired for the purpose. At Corbett's Lane Junction it made an end-on junction with the South Eastern Railway for the approaches to London Bridge. In 1846 the London & Croydon merged with the London & Brighton Railway to form the London, Brighton & South Coast Railway (LBSCR). This became one of the major railway companies operating in the south of England and retained its separate identity until it merged as part of the Southern Railway at the Grouping in 1923.

Atmospheric working

This railway was one of the few to take an interest in the atmospheric system of traction in an attempt to reduce working costs. The principle was defined in a patent to Clegg and Samuda in 1838. Briefly, it consisted of traction by atmospheric pressure acting on a piston running in an iron tube mounted between the rails. This was connected to the leading vehicle of a train by a vertical arm through a continuous slotted flap valve. Stationary engines at intervals exhausted the air in the tube ahead of the piston so that it, and therefore the train, moved forward. The slot in the top of the tube had to be covered by a flap made of short sections of well-greased leather to make the tube airtight, the flap being moved aside ahead of the arm of the piston and replaced afterwards.

The trial took place on the line from London Bridge to Croydon for local traffic. It was not a success. Opening in October 1845 for public use, all traffic had reverted to steam haulage by May 1847. It did, however, have two lasting consequences, which were needed to keep the local trains thus powered apart from the longer-distance ones. One was the construction of an 'atmospheric relief line' between New Cross Gate and West Croydon, and the other was the construction of one of the first railway flyovers, in the Norwood Junction area. A 15-inch-diameter pipe situated between the rails is a considerable embarrassment when it comes to junctions of any description!

The inherent conflicts between services with different stopping patterns and thus different performance characteristics were therefore recognised, even with traffic levels much lower than they are today.

The result was the classic and expensive but also effective response of separating them physically as far as possible. This line is now conventionally four-tracked, with tracks paired by direction.

Development

The Brighton's station at London Bridge now has nine platforms (8-16), though rebuilding would reduce these to six. It is complete with its own approach roads and is operated more or less as a separate railway from the South Eastern alongside. Over the initial section until the South London and Tulse Hill lines diverge, there are no fewer than 11 parallel running lines. All are carried on arches above street level and on these can be seen a continuous kaleidoscope of railway activity.

The first station reached is New Cross Gate, where there are platforms on all four running lines, plus what was then the East London bay on the down side. Conventional pairs of side platforms at subsequent stations on the slow lines at each side of the formation follow, until the extensive station at Norwood Junction is reached.

There is a steep 1 in 100 climb over the couple of miles from New Cross Gate to Forest Hill, but the rest is more or less level. Successively, there are stations at Brockley, Honor Oak Park, Forest Hill and Sydenham. After this, a flying junction takes the branch to Crystal Palace, 7m 61ch from London Bridge, off the down slow and over the main line. There is a corresponding spur in the up direction.

The main line continues, with stations at Penge West and Anerley. Flying junctions then bring in the line from Victoria via West Norwood and that from Tulse Hill, both via Crystal Palace.

Multiple running lines south of Norwood Junction lead in all possible directions, mostly with grade separation. In the present context the line to West Croydon (10m 35ch from London Bridge) is of two

tracks, and a single north-facing bay platform is available there. The south-end bay which was used by the service from Wimbledon has now been filled in, as this service is now part of London Tramlink.

Signalling as far as Forest Hill is by the London Bridge power box (1975), the remainder by Three Bridges (1983).

Electrification

On 25 March 1928, DC electric services were introduced between London Bridge and Crystal Palace Low Level, and all other Southern services in the area under consideration were either newly electrified or had their system converted from AC to DC by the end of 1929. The third rail has proved to be an enduring means of railway traction.

Though not affecting this area directly, the completion of the comprehensive Kent Coast electrification schemes of 1959 and 1961 eliminated steam traction from passenger services, with all since being powered by electricity and just the occasional diesel multiple-unit.

Above: The down side of Norwood Junction offers ticket barriers and machines followed by a dreary subway in best Brighton tradition, but not much else. The door on the left is open in this picture of 12 April 2010, but the overall impression given is 'closed'. How can stations become more welcoming in appearance? John Glover

Left: This, the up side, seen on 12 April 2010, is the business part of Norwood Junction station, where considerable efforts have been made in recent years to tidy it all up. Note in particular the paved and direct route in for passengers. John Glover

CHAPTER 8: **ROLLING STOCK**

Right: *The Siemens stock for the North London Railway ended up on the Lancaster, Morecambe and Heysham line, converted to AC overhead operation for experimental purposes. As such, it saw the line out until closure. This is Morecambe station in December 1965. Amazingly, the trains needed to reverse twice in a journey of less than eight miles, which took around 25 minutes. Relatively few services though covered the final stretch from Morecambe to Heysham. Electrail Collection (6331)*

The rolling stock used on this group of services over the years is now considered, up to the delivery of the new trains for London Overground, which arrived from 2009.

South London line, London Bridge to Victoria

The South London 1909 AC electric trains were made up of coaches of open compartment type with a side gangway, but there were no vestibule connections throughout the train. The stock was 60ft long and 9ft wide, with a chocolate and cream livery, and a unit set comprised one Driving Motor Coach and a Driving Trailer. They carried 112 Third Class passengers and 12 First. There were four 150hp motors in each motor coach, which received current transformed to 600V on the coach itself. Current collection was by overhead bow collector, with duplicate contacts. The contact surface was a renewable aluminium strip and each motor coach had twin bows to suit opposing directions of travel. Either or both bows could be raised or dropped by compressed air from the brake system, or pumped in by hand if the reservoirs were empty, as they were likely to be at the start of the day.

Power was obtained from the London Electric Supply Corporation at Deptford, and fed to the system at Queens Road Peckham, at 6,600V. The car sheds and works were built in the junction angle at Peckham Rye.

Willesden Junction-Earls Court

The trains for this service consisted of four three-car units, made up of Driving Motor, Trailer and Driving Trailer. They had Siemens electrical equipment in the body of the Driving Motor vehicle. End vestibules with end doors only were provided and seating was a mixture of longitudinal and transverse. As built, the trains had gangways between the vehicles, but these were removed in 1935. Seating was arranged as shown in Table 8.1, which provides an interesting commentary on the social values of the time, with 23% of the accommodation given over to First Class passengers, while smoking was permitted in only a third of all seats.

These trains became redundant after services were suspended in 1940 and were later withdrawn altogether. The stock, particularly the Driving Motors, was substantially rebuilt in 1951 for operating experimentally on the Lancaster, Morecambe and Heysham line at 50

Table 8.1: Seating in new electric trains for Willesden-Earls Court services

	First Class	Unclassed	Total	
DM	-	40	40	Smoking
T	16	-	16	Smoking
	22	28	50	Non-smoking
DT	-	60	60	Non-smoking
Totals	38	128	166	

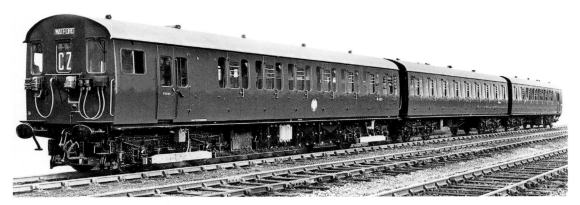

Above: *The use of slam doors on the LMS compartment stock made the loading and unloading of trains rather quicker than with their predecessors, but they were phased out and eventually replaced by the 1957 stock. A set of six cars approaches Headstone Lane station with empty stock for Broad Street on 6 April 1963. L. Sandler*

Left: *This is the plain-greenliveried three-car set of what would later become Class 501. Running trials began in March 1957 and they were introduced in service on 27 May. They were known by the exciting title of LM (for London Midland Region) DC London sets. The three window bars made them unmistakable. Ian Allan Library*

cycles AC overhead but at 6,600V. Pantographs were fitted and all seating became one class only. This was part of the British Railways investigation on whether to rescind the long-standing decision to standardise future electrification schemes at 1,500V DC overhead with 25kV AC, as eventually happened.

The four trains were finally retired with the closure of the Heysham line on 3 January 1966.

North London and Watford DC services

Electrification work was completed in 1922, with the electricity coming from an LNWR power station at Stonebridge Park, which fed 11 substations.

For the completed scheme, many more trains were required. These took the general specification of the Siemens units outlined above and were built between 1915 and 1924. Electrical equipment was supplied by the Swiss firm Oerlikon (the district of Zurich in

which the company is situated), and it was by this name that the trains became known.

The general layout with open saloons was very similar; what distinguished both these types of trains from later offerings was the use of large windows in the passenger saloons and the lack of doors. 'The layout looked rather like a bus, but the extensive use of wood inside gave them the appearance of a small chapel' was the opinion of railway writer R. L. Vickers.

These vehicles were made up of Driving Motor Brake, Trailer and Driving Trailer and were equipped with the Westinghouse air brake. As built, the maximum speed in service was 45mph and the rate of acceleration a modest 1.3 to 1.4mph per second.

It would seem that these trains were much liked for their riding qualities, and they were described as 'the smoothest-riding and most comfortable suburban electric stock ever to run in this country' (O. S. Nock, 1960). A three-car train did, however, weigh a fairly

Above: The interiors of the saloons in the 1957 Class 501 units were of a design type well known to those who experienced that era, but this view is included here to show just what could be done within a standard body shell. Compartments were the same, except that the seating was six across, rather than 3+2 as here, and with a partition between each of them. They were all Second (later Standard) class. British Railways, Ian Allan Library

massive 112 tons. 'These trains roll along with a slight and pleasant swing and with a marked absence of jolts and jerks' (Linecar, 1947). Praise indeed.

In 1922 the LNWR electric stock comprised 80 Motor Coaches and 144 Trailers. Withdrawals started in 1956.

Compartment stock

These trains were not enough, however, and following the 1923 Grouping the London Midland & Scottish Railway introduced compartment stock in an attempt to boost capacity. The 25 sets were built in two batches, in 1927 and 1933, and thus had a substantially different layout, as Table 8.2 shows.

It will be noted that while the First Class numbers remained virtually static, the total accommodation as measured by seats rose by 114. This is getting on for a 70% increase, and demonstrates the flexibility that designers can have within a body shell that was of almost constant size throughout. Of note in this design was the 'slam doors to all compartments' approach, and that those compartments sat six a side, or five a side in First Class. One undeniable benefit was the speed at which trains of this sort could load and unload passengers, though slickness of operation did depend on the last passenger in or out shutting the door.

What this achieved was to seat as many people as possible, but it was mostly extremely uncomfortable

for those who still had to stand. If you were too short to reach the luggage racks to hang on to, there wasn't anything else away from the doors apart from other people's knees. Compared with the earlier builds these trains were anything but spacious, but they served a purpose. They too lasted until the 1957 stock was delivered.

First Class accommodation on London suburban services was withdrawn as a wartime economy to maximise the space available for all.

With all these earlier types of LMS rolling stock and that of its constituents, one marker light in each corner of the front ends was used to give route indications. This allowed 15 combinations in total, using one, two, three or four of them illuminated, but never none. On a fairly compact system such as the North London lines, different codes were used for trains terminating intermediately, and also for empty trains according to their destinations. All these train types carried a prominent destination blind for the benefit of passengers.

Class 501

The generic description London Area DC services of the London Midland Region of British Railways comfortably covered a multitude of operations. By the post-war years all the original rolling stock was becoming time-expired, and a uniform new fleet was to be provided. The vehicles were built at the Southern Region's Eastleigh Works from 1957, and bore a strong general resemblance to the British Railways-designed Southern EPB sets as well as the locomotive-hauled suburban coaches then in production. Also, they were all on the short 57-foot underframes, whereas 64 feet was universal on the Southern. Thus the intermediate trailers had nine compartments, as against the ten in their Southern counterparts.

The Eastleigh units were constructed as part of the 1955 Modernisation Plan. Later Class 501, these 57 trains comprised Driving Motor Open Brake Second, Trailer Compartment Second and a Driving Trailer Open Brake Second. They were made up to six cars as necessary.

In conception they were very similar to the inner-suburban Southern Region stock, which they resembled closely; the main differences were the use of the shorter underframe to cope more easily with the substantial curvature they needed to negotiate, the use of triple bars on all droplight windows because of limited clearances, rather more jumper cables hung on their front ends than their Southern equivalents, screw couplings between units, and – very un-Southern – a destination blind. Fancy actually telling the customers where the train was going! Two-character letter/number front blinds replaced the earlier use of marker lights.

Three-car sets were an unknown formation on the Southern, and they had two guard's/luggage areas. There was one next to each cab, which provided the only access for the driver. Two sets were necessary, quoting a contemporary account, 'to keep out of the passenger compartments some of the bulky impedimenta, including mailbags'. Apparently, this was

Table 8.2: 1927 LMS compartment stock for North London and Watford services			
	First Class	Unclassed	Total
DM	-	84	84
T	40	60	100
DT	-	96	96
Totals	40	240	280

becoming a problem with the existing trains.

Notable was the continued use of the compartment layout for the centre trailers, which was still being used for their loco-hauled equivalents. These were one of the last groups of stock to include 'Ladies Only' compartments, distinguished by a green label in the window glass. The 57-foot stock allowed the provision of nine compartments; each seating six a side; this gave a very creditable total of 108 seats in the centre trailers.

The seven sets of bays in the end (driving) vehicles were divided into two separate saloons, with 3+2 seating in the intermediate bays. The saloon seat ends were inclined from the floor towards the body sides to form a centre gangway with maximum possible width at shoulder height and the widest possible seating room. Each thus carried 74 seated passengers, making 256 for the three-car unit. They were frequently, if not normally, made up to two units for six-car operation.

These trains monopolised the services on what was now the London Midland Region of British Railways from Broad Street, all day to Richmond and in the peak hours to Watford, and also those direct all day from Euston to Watford Junction. Even with the addition of the rather shaky Croxley Green branch

services, the employment of 57 units seems now a little excessive, though overprovision (by today's standards) was a common feature of the times. Maybe the expectations of the reliability in service of the trains then being built were less exacting.

This was an entirely fourth rail 630V DC operation, given the need in part to share tracks with London Underground, though converted to third rail in 1970 as already recorded. It was part of an overall drive for simplification and cost containment, another example of this being the elimination of 6.25kV AC electrification elsewhere in the London area and its replacement with 25kV AC.

Liveries

The 501s were delivered in BR EMU green, with minimal yellow lining; they were later painted all-over blue, then blue and grey. Yellow panels and later yellow ends were added as appropriate.

Compartments eventually went out of fashion, due mostly to vandalism but also to rising fears about personal safety. Mid-life refurbishment saw their conversion to open saloons.

Above: This view shows Southern EPB No 6320 having left Dalston Kingsland in a westbound direction and about to run parallel with the lines from Broad Street and Dalston Junction on the right. This is in effect the arrangement that was recreated with the new East London Railway extension to Highbury & Islington. The bridge behind the signalbox carries Boleyn Road, which required major reconstruction to enable the platforms at Dalston Kingsland to be extended to four-car length. Paul D. Shannon

Above: The shortage of Class 313 units became critical for the DC services, and to alleviate it three surplus Class 508 units were found in Merseyside and moved to Willesden. They could be used only on the Watford Junction to London Euston services, where No 508303 is seen arriving on 7 March 2005 with blind already changed. The Class 508s were built as four-car units, and the 43 'missing' trailers can still be found forming part of the Class 455/7 units of South West Trains. John Glover

Southern EPBs, Class 416/3

The next development was the inauguration of a service between Camden Road, Stratford and North Woolwich. From 1985 third rail electrification was completed all the way to North Woolwich, which became the main eastern terminus of the North London Line. Trains were needed to operate this service, and a hunt around the Southern Region for suitable stock produced 16 EPB (electro-pneumatic brake) units of Class 416/3 (Nos 6313-6328).

These two-car units were built at Eastleigh in 1959 on old 2-NOL 62ft 6in underframes, for Southern Region suburban duties. They were Second Class (later Standard Class) only, gangwayed, and seated 178 people, undergoing general refurbishment in 1979.

Each droplight window in the doors was equipped with three window bars. As with the earlier units, the impression made on passengers inside them was certainly that they were caged in, even if it wasn't downright claustrophobic.

Based at Selhurst depot (Croydon), they needed to access the North London Line on a daily basis. Short of using locomotive haulage, this could only be arranged via the connection at Richmond.

They were to monopolise the North London services for a few years until they themselves were replaced by the dual-voltage Class 313s.

Class 313s and Class 507s

The Great Northern electric services from Moorgate to Welwyn Garden City and Hertford North were inaugurated in 1976. A total of 64 Class 313 sliding-door three-car dual-voltage units, later with 202 seats and one wheelchair space, were built for this service, and were based at Hornsey. The dual capability was needed because of the change in electrification systems imposed at Drayton Park, where the line entered a tunnel formerly used by the London Transport Northern City Line and where clearances were insufficient for AC overhead equipment. These

trains therefore swapped to third rail while stationary at the platform.

Somewhat amazingly, it was later found that some units could be spared for the North London, where their dual capability was now needed, and also for the Euston-Watford services. Indeed, 23 of these trains were transferred, which suggests that the original orders for the GN were more than a little on the generous side.

As it turned out, it was stretching the point to try and run all North London and all Euston-Watford services with this fleet, and three extra and largely similar units of Class 507 were transferred from Merseyside in 2002/03. The key difference with these trains was that they were DC only, so they could only be used on the Euston-Watford services. In any event, they were stabled and maintained at Willesden.

The Class 313s continued to operate all the former LNWR London electric services until they too were displaced in 2009 and 2010 by deliveries of the Class 378 units for London Overground.

Other trains

Various types of diesel units have operated the Gospel Oak-Barking services, and also those on the West London Line prior to electrification, but these are not considered here.

Similarly, electric trains operated at various times by British Railways Southern Region in South London are too varied to warrant description.

London Overground

All rolling stock operating the services that now form London Overground has been replaced with brand new trains, consisting of Class 378 electric units and Class 172 diesel units for Gospel Oak-Barking. The new fleet consists of two varieties of Class 378 'Electrostar' EMUs built by Bombardier at Derby, both with DC capability but only one with AC as well. All the DC units are capable of being dual-fitted at a later date. These will be considered further in Chapter 17.

Above: Hackney Central lies east of the main line near Hackney Downs station, which is seen in the distance crossing the North London Line. Can a worthwhile pedestrian link be forged between the two? No 378018 is seen in bright and clean condition arriving with a service for Stratford on 10 February 2010.
John Glover

Above: *These trains, Nos 378137/44, are in the depot at New Cross Gate and were photographed from a passing service on 28 April 2010. There are extensive facilities here, and the Willesden-based trains are also sent here to undergo servicing that cannot be undertaken at that depot.* John Glover

Right: *This interior shot of the Class 378 series shows the wide gangways, the 'one-piece' appearance achieved by minimising the interruption caused by corridor connections, and the perch seats. It is only on inspection that the paucity of seating provision becomes clear at around 36 per car, depending on type.* John Glover

2

Developing The Railway

CHAPTER 9: **THE GROUPING, THEN BRITISH RAILWAYS**

Early signs

The Railways Act 1921 was also known as the Grouping Act. It brought the many smaller railways in Britain into the four main private companies of the Great Western, the Southern, the London Midland & Scottish and the London & North Eastern railways. This was to be a relatively short-lived arrangement, which took effect on 1 January 1923.

Schedule 1 of that Act listed all the railway companies that were so affected. These consisted of 27 constituent companies of the main groups, and 93 subsidiary companies. Thus the LNWR was a constituent of the LMS, but the North London Line was a subsidiary of the LNWR.

There was, however, one substantial omission, and that was the Metropolitan Railway. Was it, or was it not, a main-line company, then penetrating territory 50 miles distant from Baker Street? It was not, and was thus included as part of the Underground when the London Passenger Transport Board (LPTB) was created on 1 July 1933. What might have happened if the 'Met'

had become part of (probably) the LNER is another matter. It might be that this would have put a rather different complexion on the relationships between the 'Big Four' main-line companies and the Underground, and their successors. Maybe all the subsurface lines of the Underground would fit more happily with London Overground than the deep-level tube railways?

As it was, the later 1930s saw the adoption of revenue pooling, in which receipts were shared out in agreed proportions between the participants. These included the buses, trolleybuses and trams, and took some of the tensions out of joint arrangements. These included the Underground taking over, electrifying and operating selected LNER routes (in particular). This work was completed, although not as extensively as originally intended, in the early post-war period.

Post-war

In the closing years of the Second World War considerable official thought was given to post-war reconstruction and what might be needed. However,

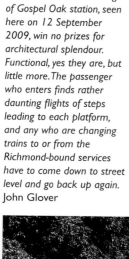

Below: The street buildings of Gospel Oak station, seen here on 12 September 2009, win no prizes for architectural splendour. Functional, yes they are, but little more. The passenger who enters finds rather daunting flights of steps leading to each platform, and any who are changing trains to or from the Richmond-bound services have to come down to street level and go back up again.
John Glover

nearly all this work was related to travel to and from central London, and non-radial routes received little attention. Some modest references were made to the needs of freight and proposals to turn over the north side of the Circle Line for that purpose, but the work of these years can be discarded for present purposes.

Twenty-five years after the Grouping, on 1 January 1948, the 'Big Four' companies were nationalised under the Transport Act 1947. Henceforward, they would be part of British Railways. The 1947 Act also nationalised the LPTB, and both were part of the British Transport Commission.

This structure lasted until 1 January 1963, when the Transport Act 1962 made each of them Boards in their own right, thus lessening the ties between them.

Beeching, 1963

How was the railway itself faring? The reality was that non-radial rail services, in those days anyway, were not basic components of London's passenger transport system. They certainly had a use, but the numbers carried were not in the top league, and there were other more pressing needs to be met. They also had a less than satisfactory financial performance. Of this, Dr Richard (later Lord) Beeching was in little doubt. In his 'Reshaping' report of 1963, the following passenger services in the London area were targeted for withdrawal. Their subsequent fate is also indicated:

Clapham Junction to Kensington Olympia
    Now part of London Overground
Kentish Town (as it then was) to Barking
    Now part of London Overground
London Broad Street (as it then was) to Richmond
    Now part of London Overground
Watford Junction to Croxley Green
    Last train 1996; last bus replacement 2003
Romford to Upminster
    Electrified at 25kV AC
Watford Junction to St Albans Abbey
    Electrified at 25kV AC; proposed in 2009
    for conversion to light rail
Harrow & Wealdstone to Belmont
    Withdrawn 1964
Seven Sisters to Palace Gates
    Withdrawn 1963
West Drayton to Staines West
    Withdrawn 1965
West Drayton to Uxbridge Vine Street
    Withdrawn 1962
Woodside to Sanderstead
    Withdrawn 1983; much later most became
    part of London Tramlink

Note that in those days there were no passenger services at all between Dalston and Stratford or between Kensington Olympia and Willesden Junction.

With a slightly less drastic prescription, the stopping services between Euston and Broad Street to Watford

Above: *Passengers at Bushey in the autumn of 1978 await the arrival of a Euston-bound six-car formation of Class 501 units. As the condition of the fourth rail shows, it is still in use for British Rail and Underground trains alike. Until 1974 the station was named Bushey & Oxhey.*
John Glover

Above: *The view from the east side across the outer platform ends at Liverpool Street on 22 August 1967. A Class 47 still in two-tone green heads a Norwich train in Platform 9 and the resident Class 15 station pilot, No D8234, can also be seen. Beyond is the Broad Street viaduct, the much higher level of which can readily be appreciated. The signalbox is visible, as well as a Class 08 diesel shunter. Behind the wall in the middle distance, the two sets of railway premises were separated by the narrow Sun Street Passage, which still exists and was connected then to the bridge on the right. It was about the only item in the area at ground level.* John Glover

Junction were to be 'modified'. Quite what this meant was not specified, but at that time the Bakerloo Line extended from Queen's Park to Watford Junction.

It appeared that services from the Great Northern line to Broad Street would continue, as indeed they did until displaced by the GN electrification.

Thus some of the core operations of what was to become London Overground were perhaps lucky to survive at all. It should perhaps be stressed here that while the British Railways Board (as was) could put up a case for service closure, the decision on whether or not to sanction this was the responsibility of the Minister of Transport.

Economics

It is worth recalling the words of the 'Reshaping' report in terms of what it called London services as a whole: 'In essence the problem is this. The capacity of the system ... is limited by physical restrictions ... which could be removed only at high cost... The level of fares is too low to finance costly increases in system capacity, but the demand goes on getting heavier.'

In other words, there wasn't a business case to expand the infrastructure to accommodate more train services half a century ago. That was to come later in social cost benefit analysis and other methods of measuring social worth. If the infrastructure is there and available you might be able to run a train service profitably, or at least with minimal losses, but the overheads of what are now termed track access charges would cripple the operation financially. More track needed? Forget it!

Greater London Council, 1970

On 1 January 1970 the Greater London Council assumed control of a newly created London Transport Executive, minus its Country Bus and Green Line operations. The GLC's brief was as set out as follows:

1. It shall be the general duty of the Greater London Council to develop policies, and to encourage, organise and, where appropriate, carry out measures, which will promote the provision of integrated, efficient and economic transport facilities and services for Greater London.

Tickets

Under this, the Transport (London) Act 1969, the Railways Board was placed under a duty to co-operate with the Executive, and some of the important outcomes have been discussed. Besides matters such as the restoration of passenger services from Dalston to Stratford, then to North Woolwich, together with electrification, they were to include the introduction of Thameslink in its original form and restoration of rail services between Farringdon and Blackfriars via a new City Thameslink station.

London Rail Study, 1974

This Study was set up by the Minister and the GLC, under the chairmanship of Sir David Barran. It too was concerned largely with radial services, but a useful section discussed the non-orbital routes.

The most interesting of these was Ringrail. This would involve (to quote the report) 'a frequent British Rail orbital service using principally the North, West, and South London lines, and providing interchange with every radial line. A new tunnel would be required under the Thames to complete the orbital link in East London.'

The routeing was thus that to be adopted as the basis of the London Overground orbital network, with the difference that the East London Line remained untouched. Instead, the North London route would continue east to Stratford and then south to Canning Town on the North Woolwich branch. From here there would be new

construction beneath the river, with an interchange at Maze Hill Southeastern station. Services would rejoin the South London at Lewisham and then proceed via Denmark Hill. Stratford, Highbury & Islington, West Hampstead and Willesden Junction were marked out as sites for improved interchange, with several others for new stations. Eight of these would be on the West London Line; since then, three have been built.

The projected results were not good. 'On the face of it, this is an attractive proposition ... if there is increasingly decentralisation away from central London, as the strategic centres build up in importance and attract more people to work, the pattern of demand is likely to become more diversified.' But demand was put at only 2,000-8,000 passengers in the peak hour in each direction.

'That,' said Barran, 'is by no means sufficient to justify an expensive new railway. Furthermore, stopping the trains on radial routes to give interchange with orbital services would cause considerable loss of time to passengers on the radial routes and would cause increased operating problems, loss of line capacity (causing overcrowding for existing passengers) and extra costs.'

Perhaps unsurprisingly, the scheme was omitted from the report's recommendations.

Another scheme evaluated was a low-cost (but also a lower-benefit) alternative. This ignored most of the network south of the river, concentrating on offering

Above: South Acton is an uncomplicated and modest wayside station, the Underground shuttle from Acton Town having ceased in 1959. The platform for this was located to the left of this view of May 1978, but nothing remains. Then there were semaphores, and a Class 501 unit on a Broad Street-Richmond service in Rail Blue livery will shortly depart. John Glover

Above: *The opening of West London Line platforms at West Brompton in 1999, with the ability to make a quick change to the District Line adjacent, also enabled use to be made of the same ticket office facilities. The Underground station is seen to the right, and behind are Earls Court 2 (left) and Earls Court 1 (right). This northfacing photograph was taken in June 1999.* John Glover

diesel services every 20 minutes which would run between Greenford, Ealing Broadway, Willesden Junction, Gospel Oak, Stratford and North Woolwich, and Clapham Junction, Willesden Junction, Gospel Oak and Barking. Broad Street-Richmond services would remain unchanged.

An electrified version was also evaluated, but with no better results. In the event, diesel services between Camden Road, Dalston, Stratford and North Woolwich were to become a reality, and were later electrified.

Also of interest, the Barran report carefully skirted around the subject of the organisation needed to take the various proposals forward. 'Only if the [minor co-ordination changes suggested] fail to live up to our expectations should a basic reorganisation be contemplated.'

Fares and ticketing

Another development of the GLC days was the introduction of the zonal fares system and the introduction of the Travelcard. Under this arrangement, the whole of Greater London was

divided into six broadly concentric fares zones, and fares were based on the number of zones through which the passenger travelled. This was a vast simplifying exercise, and services operated by British Rail also issued (and accepted) Travelcard season tickets. This did, however, not extend to ordinary single and return tickets, which were not included universally until January 2010.

It was the court case arising from the 'Fares Fair' initiative, under which fares were kept at such a level that some thought represented an unreasonable burden on the local taxpayer, that brought about the wresting away of London Transport from the GLC. This became law in the London Regional Transport Act 1984 and transfer took place rather hurriedly on 29 June of that year.

Once again the successor to London Transport became a Ministerial responsibility. Still the uncomfortable nature of the BR/LRT relationship continued, but the 1983 White Paper (Public Transport in London) did no more than raise the possibilities of change. The ability of LRT to make grants to British Rail was strengthened.

Above: A Freightliner train with a negligible load passes through Hackney Wick behind No 90144 on 11 November 1998. This line went from no passenger service to diesel multiple-unit operation, then to electric third rail (as here), but also with overhead for freight. The 25kV AC now suffices for both. John Glover

Left: A Class 501 unit in Rail Blue livery leaves West Hampstead station on 1 December 1978 with a Broad Street service. Like their Southern Region counterparts these were functional workaday trains, with virtually nothing in the way of frills. How else could they seat so many passengers? John Glover

CHAPTER 10: **SETTING THE SCENE**

Above: *Shoreditch London Underground station is now closed permanently, but is seen here in better days on 16 June 2003. The Pedley Street location was not that obvious for those who didn't know it was there, although it was close to the centre of Shoreditch life. To what extent do such matters affect patronage levels?* John Glover

Right: *Shoreditch platform, looking towards Liverpool Street, on 16 June 2003. The stop markers are well in advance of the end of the line, which in this case means that passengers have to walk that much further to reach the staircase. Through the lush vegetation beyond, it was occasionally possible to see a train on the main line.* John Glover

The next major development was the privatisation of the national rail network. Though its form subsequently underwent substantial modifications, the principles remained largely unchanged.

Railways Act, 1993

This, the principal privatisation Act as far as the national railway system is concerned, needs little introduction. The key principles were:

* the separation of railway operation from infrastructure provision

* the competitive letting of passenger franchises as operational contracts with defined duties, for set periods of time
* the negotiation by operators with the network provider for the provision of train paths, for which they then pay
* the hiving off of rolling stock provision to separate companies (ROSCOs)
* the creation of a rail regulatory body
* open access for freight operators and (in theory) passenger operators.

This was in many ways an extension of the situation as it was developing under public ownership, which was summarised as 'being run within clear objectives and tight financial disciplines … making services more attractive and travelling easier for the public, and generally to cut costs in the interests of the taxpayer and the fare payer'. This quote comes from the 1983 White Paper of a decade earlier.

Greater London Authority

The tone of these years emphasised the geographical devolution of government, and the results in Scotland and Wales are widely recognised. Yet Greater London has a larger population than either (about 7.9 million), and here too devolution was happening.

The demise of the Greater London Council left an uncomfortable political vacuum; who was able to speak for the capital as a whole? So, 15 years or so after abolition, the Labour government's Greater London Authority (GLA) Act 1999 created a new authority. Briefly, the Mayor was given the duty to produce an Integrated Transport Strategy 'for the promotion and encouragement of safe, integrated, efficient and economic transport services to, from and within Greater London'.

The Act also established Transport for London as a corporate body with wide and extensive powers subject to the Mayor's directions and guidance. In particular, it was able to secure or provide public transport services and had a mutual duty to co-operate with the Strategic Rail Authority (SRA). This was, however, subject to the caveat that the SRA could reject proposals that would interfere unacceptably with national rail services into and out of London, or would increase the cost of services to the national taxpayer. The Greater London Authority sets fares and service levels for all services provided by Transport for London.

Transport for London

The creation of Transport for London (TfL) represented a return of what was once London Transport to local political control, though the new body had considerably wider interests. It was created in 2000 under s154 of the GLA Act. Directly accountable to the Mayor, at present Boris Johnson, TfL is a functional body of the Authority, responsible for implementing the Mayor's transport strategy and managing transport services (of all sorts) across the capital.

It is not an organisation that can afford to stand still. Projections of population growth are that, compared with 2000, there will be 700,000 additional people living and working in London by 2016, with the population of around 7.3 million in 2000 rising to 8.1 million. That offers a considerable challenge in terms of growing

travel demands. In the year 2010/11 the Underground carried 1,107 million passengers, an all-time record. Projections suggest that by 2016 this could rise by 15%, or about 3.4 million passengers each and every day.

There are several principal TfL companies with public transport responsibilities related to rail. London Underground Ltd is responsible for operating the Underground network and owns 260 stations. Docklands Light Railway Ltd owns the land on which the DLR is built and is responsible for the operation of the railway.

Transport Trading Ltd is the holding company for all TfL's operating transport companies, and receives revenues from the sales of Travelcards and similar in connection with all forms of transport operated by TfL. By law, TfL can only carry out certain activities through a limited liability company that is a TfL subsidiary, or which TfL formed alone or with others. Rail for London Ltd (London Rail) is one such subsidiary; another is the London Transport Museum.

Above: The eastern end of the Kensal Green twin tunnels (320 yards) on the DC lines, which abut the platforms, give the appearance of being of relatively small diameter and suited to tube train operation. Bakerloo Line services (one of which may just be seen having left the far end of the nearer tunnel) do of course operate here, but so too do Watford DC full-size vehicles. The date is 7 May 2008. John Glover

Left: These are the platforms at Rotherhithe on 26 April 2006, facing south towards Surrey Quays, where some daylight penetrates to the track. The narrowness of the platforms and the limitations that this would put on their use by large numbers of people is apparent. John Glover

Above: Two of Stratford's Class 105 DMUs call at Hackney Wick station on 21 July 1980. This view, looking east from the footbridge, shows the relatively basic nature of the then new station and also the trademark white roof front end that Stratford applied to its fleet – in one case but not the other. There is no sign as yet of electrification; that was still a few years away. John Glover

London Rail

London Rail was established in 2003, with the objectives of raising standards by focusing investment in London's railways and to develop a more integrated approach to rail governance. The Railways Act 2005 gave greater responsibility for rail in London to TfL and transferred services on the Overground network to that body.

London Rail is discussed fully, later.

The Mayor's objectives

There are many other projects in which the Mayor is taking an interest. Beyond the current investment programme, even with the introduction of Crossrail and Thameslink, crowding on the London Underground network will remain. Any potential schemes will have

to be subject to a thorough value for money and feasibility analysis and will have to be considered in light of any future funding constraints.

The Mayor intends to seek longer-term enhancements and extensions, including:

* Northern Line Upgrade 2, which includes partial line separation to increase line capacity significantly, especially through the City
* A privately funded Northern Line extension to Battersea to support regeneration of the Battersea/Nine Elms area
* A Bakerloo Line southern extension to create a new south-east to north-west strategic route, freeing up National Rail capacity at London Bridge.

More generally, the Mayor's draft planning (as opposed to transport) document had this to say:

The Mayor will work with strategic partners to improve the public transport system in London, including cross-London and orbital rail links to support future development and regeneration priority areas, and increase public transport capacity by:

* implementing Crossrail, the Mayor's top strategic transport priority for London
* completing upgrades to and extending the London Underground network
* implementing a high-frequency Londonwide service on the national rail network
* enhancing the different elements of the London Overground network to implement an orbital rail network
* completing the Thameslink programme
* developing the Chelsea-Hackney line (Crossrail 2) later in the plan period
* improving the reliability, quality and safety of inter-regional rail services, including domestic services for commuters, while safeguarding services within London.

Right: This was Fork Junction, with one line diverging to the right, though it would be hard to guess that in this 2001 view of a Richmond-North Woolwich service arriving at Stratford Low Level formed of No 313107. Vegetation can quickly recolonise abandoned bits of railway. John Glover

Left: *The 1999 bus station at Canada Water is to all intents the surface entrance to the two Underground and two Overground platforms below. This is June 2003, so both then had Underground services. London Overground has many benefits as a choice of name, but one might pity the staff in explaining that what used to be Underground is now Overground but is still in the same place, which is underground!* John Glover

Franchising

Before TfL came on the scene, services on the National Rail network were part of what had become the normal franchised operations. Those north of the Thames, which are now part of London Overground, together with the West London Line to Clapham Junction, were part of the Silverlink network run by National Express. It was already effectively two sets of services, latterly Silverlink County and Silverlink Metro. The Metro part comprised the local services south of Watford Junction, which were a separate entity from the AC services anyway, together with the line to Barking. When the Silverlink franchise expired on 10 November 2007, the County operations were incorporated into a new franchise, with parts of what was Central Trains. This is now operated by London Midland, a Govia company.

South of the Thames, the National Rail services concerned were operated by Southern, also part of Govia. This franchise was retendered and Govia retained the revised contract; the renewal became effective on 20 September 2009.

Railway powers

There was much more in the 1999 Act to strengthen the Mayor's hand, but what did he (then Ken Livingstone) want to achieve? The Strategy document of July 2001 had this to say:

The Transport Strategy sets the objective of establishing a London Metro service with the following core elements:

* Services styled, branded and marketed as an urban Metro
* 'Turn up and go' frequency (ie a target minimum 10-minute frequency throughout the day should be the norm)
* Services integrated with the Underground and bus networks

* Fares and ticketing arrangements for individual journeys integrated with the Underground, and other TfL and National Rail services
* London Metro services that meet agreed standards and improved levels of passenger facilities, including standards of passenger information, and are progressively being made accessible for all
* Stations that meet security criteria.

Services meeting these requirements would be included on an integrated London Metro map alongside the Underground. A planned programme of improvements to stations and services may be required to meet all the above standards, including the target frequency, fares structure, levels of security and accessibility to the system.

The London orbital network of the North, West, South and East London (then London Underground) lines together with the Barking to Gospel Oak line should form the core of a wider London orbital network. This would be achieved by building on the services operated over the existing network, with service and interchange enhancements and with additional, overlapping services from adjacent lines, to

Below: *Dalston Kingsland station has now been in place for the best part of thirty years and the entrance from Kingsland High Street is difficult to pass by without noticing, as seen here on 12 September 2009. This is undoubtedly a well-sited station for the centre of Dalston; would that similar statements were always true.* John Glover

create London Metro standards of service and facilities. Improved interchange, especially at stations served by both orbital and radial services, would be a key feature. This would require new infrastructure.

Such a network has the potential to provide for many journeys with both origins and destinations in inner and outer London and beyond, for which public transport options are currently limited. It can provide an alternative for cross-London journeys by public transport to travelling via central London, and could serve gateway stations to areas of regeneration.

What happened?

That, essentially, is how London Overground has developed subsequently. Notable in the above and the accompanying diagram in the Mayor's Plan is the lack of any reference to the Watford-Euston DC line, while the North London is shown as heading firmly for North Woolwich. Northern extensions of the East London are shown both to Willesden Junction via Primrose Hill (which link nowadays has no passenger service, although there is a nice new terminating platform ready for it at the Low Level station) and to Finsbury Park via Canonbury. This again has no passenger rail service nowadays, and to reach it trains would need to cross the North London AC lines on the level by a newly provided set of crossings.

South of the river, Wimbledon is shown as a proposed extension from Peckham Rye via Tulse Hill, but Clapham Junction is only a possible future extension. The other termini of New Cross, West Croydon and Crystal Palace remain unchanged.

There was one further matter to be resolved. With

the demise of the Strategic Rail Authority under the Railways Act 2005, which passed the responsibility for franchising to the Department for Transport (DfT), the path was eased for Transport for London to exercise similar functions for what was now to be known as London railway passenger services. These are defined in the Act as those carrying passengers wholly within Greater London, or between places within Greater London and places outside. Specifically, the restriction on TfL for funding franchise-type agreements was removed.

That done, the next move would come with the expiry and thus renewal of franchise agreements for Silverlink and for Southern. The renewal process in each case separated out those services that were to become subject to the concession agreement and named London Overground.

An interesting addition in the 2005 Act was the need for the Mayor to ensure that at least two members of TfL should represent railway passenger interests outside Greater London. This perhaps reflects the long-running funding and fares problems associated with those parts of the Underground outside Greater London which are in Hertfordshire and Buckinghamshire, and to some extent in Essex.

Freight traffic

The collection of lines that today makes up London Overground is not an easy one to operate. That is not surprising, given the historical perspective, as they were built by different companies at different times and any ideas of co-operation were perhaps modest. Yet there were links, and the ambitions of the London

& North Western Railway to reach the City and the docks has already been discussed. Also, the West London Line was never intended as a north/south link across the western end of the capital, but it was a role that it found and was successfully exploited. South of the river generally, the conflicts of accessing both the West End and the City produced what appears at first sight to be excessive duplication, but the logic is there. As for the East London, another link across the Thames it may have been, but the Brunels and their financial backers certainly never saw it as a railway link.

The common thread that comes out of this is that these are general-purpose railways, in the best (or worst) sense of the term. Historically, given the effective exclusion of freight traffic crossing central London, more peripheral ways had to be found of achieving this objective. Combinations of the North, West and South London lines were the principal means of so doing. The East London Line, too, carried freight, but rail access was so tortuous and the gradients sufficiently steep that freight traffic was never carried to any real extent.

It is also perhaps relevant to consider what happens to freight if it doesn't use the North London line, and in this is included the Gospel Oak-Barking line. As of today, and with the East Coast ports in mind particularly, the next possible circumferential routeing around London is via Ely, Peterborough, Leicester and Nuneaton, for the Midlands and North. How does one get to Ely? It is possible from the former Great Eastern, providing paths can be found through Stratford to reach Cambridge, or via Ipswich for traffic from Felixstowe or Harwich.

Cross-London alternatives

From the former London, Tilbury & Southend territory it is far more difficult. The main and effectively the only rail exit for industries and ports in the North Thames area is via Barking and the series of flyovers so expensively constructed (but rightly so) in the late 1950s. They connect admirably with the Tottenham & Hampstead line to Gospel Oak, or less well via Forest Gate Junction to Stratford and the North London via Dalston. 'Less well' reflects the need then to cross, successively, all four running tracks of the Great Eastern main line on the level, reaching Stratford station and then turning to the north-west onto the North London.

The Tottenham & Hampstead link is fine now that it has been upgraded; although not electrified, it gives a direct link onto the North London Line and thence to Willesden via Hampstead Heath. It is, though, possible to reach the Midland main line by leaving the Tottenham & Hampstead at Junction Road Junction (lovely name!) before reaching Carlton Road Junction. Running thence via Cricklewood Curve and the Acton branch, this Midland 'Dudding Hill' link can also be used to access the Great Western at Acton Wells Junction, but only after a short sojourn on the North London in the Acton area to reach it.

Above: Hampstead Heath's ticket office and station entrance is in a busy part of the local area, as can be seen here on 12 September 2009. The station overall is but a shadow of its former self, having been the subject of post-war reconstruction. John Glover

Left: How things might be? This sign appeared on the new footbridge at Highbury & Islington, where it was photographed on 28 June 2010. Platforms 1 and 2 were then some way short of completion, but what happened to Platforms 3, 4, 5 and 6? They are for the Victoria Line and the First Capital Connect services and are hiding underground. You have to go down to one of the platforms here, up to the bridge at the other end of the station and then down by escalator/stairs to get anywhere near them. John Glover

From Barking, Forest Gate Junction and Stratford it is possible to continue round to the north via Temple Mills and the Lea Valley to Cambridge and Ely, but this is a much less direct route to the Midlands than keeping on the North London to Willesden and thence the West Coast Main Line. If the traffic is for Bristol or South Wales, the North London can be followed beyond Willesden Junction High Level and on to Acton Wells Junction, where a spur leads directly onto to the Great Western main line. Southampton can be reached via yet more of the North London to South Acton Junction and Kew Bridge, thence to Woking. Or, for destinations more directly south, the West London Line's connections via Clapham Junction will take freight trains to just about everywhere else.

The reader will appreciate the complexity of the situation, and that each of the alternatives mentioned has disbenefits as well as benefits. There is also the little matter of the capacity of each of the sections of line, and their ability to absorb both freight and passenger trains without causing undue delay to either.

SETTING THE SCENE

Above: The neat and modestly sized station building at Harlesden was photographed on 28 June 2008. This is one of the better examples on the DC lines, which do not in general excel in their overall appearance. John Glover

The TfL view

Where does that take us? The problem that it highlights is that freight traffic also has its place on the railway system today, and that its needs are as pressing as those of the passenger. This discussion has been framed in terms of through traffic in search of a route that it can use, but equally there is the traffic that has its origin or destination in Greater London. That is even more specific in terms of the route it must take in order to reach its ultimate destination.

In 2007 Transport for London produced a lengthy Rail Freight Strategy. This seemed to make all the right noises about its promotion and the finding of suitable terminals, but in the present context it pointed out that 'of the total freight serving London, rail tonnage makes up approximately 6%'. It then lauded the importance for London of construction materials and quarried stone by rail, and also the movement of municipal solid waste. Then the uncomfortable bit: 'The majority of rail freight in London is travelling through the city and doesn't serve it directly ... strategic solutions are required.'

That translated into a disinclination to accept it as a London problem. The answer from this source was to move freight by any other route possible, so that lines like the North London could be freed for local passenger services and freight that has no alternative.

Productive use

Another result of the present situation is that line capacity is at a premium and it follows that it must be used as productively as possible. Some might argue that freight can be relegated to the small hours when passenger traffic is at a low ebb, perhaps even to vanishing point, but much freight is time-sensitive too in a competitive world. If a road haulier is prepared to meet the customer's demand in terms of delivery times, so too must the railway freight company. The latter might reasonably argue, not very seriously perhaps, that freight should have the prime daytime slots, and that the passenger traffic should be carried during the night. Whose business is more important?

This is not a problem that this book will attempt to solve, and in any event time needs to be set aside for ordinary infrastructure maintenance. That too has to be factored into the requirements for an efficient working railway.

The East London scheme

The overall East London scheme dates from 1985, when it was seen as a fully integrated Metro-cum-City Crossrail. On its creation, the Strategic Rail Authority took over the interests of the Department for Transport and it became a joint venture with Transport

for London. The scope of the project in the past was not clearly defined.

It may be noted here that the purposes of the SRA as set out in s205 of the Transport Act 2000 were as follows:

* To promote the use of the railway network for the carriage of passengers and goods
* To secure the development of the railway network
* To contribute to the development of an integrated system of transport of passengers and goods

The basis of the East London upgrade has always been clear: use the existing East London Line of the Underground as the in-town section, and extend it at both ends. In the north, this would result in a new station in the Bishopsgate area (replacing the Shoreditch London Underground station), the line then joining the old Broad Street-Dalston Junction formation. Trains would then call at a reincarnated Dalston Junction and terminate at Highbury & Islington.

To the south, a number of alternatives were pursued. But all would continue over the tracks of National Rail. Here, it was considered, eight-car trains were really the minimum that could be contemplated, for line capacity reasons.

Going back to the days when the short-lived Strategic Rail Authority was in charge of this project, there were problems at a number of stations. Most notable was Wapping, in making the platforms long enough for what was then envisaged as eight-car trains. The platforms here are of minimal width, front to back, and access includes substantial and awkward flights of

stairs, placed at the southern end of the platforms. These would also be costly to lengthen, to the extent that the work needed to accommodate eight-car trains, together with making this single station Disability Discrimination Act compliant, would have cost roundly £100 million.

A not dissimilar situation occurred at Rotherhithe, while at Whitechapel the station is situated in a deep cutting. Here the platform lengths, although then partly disused, could be made sufficient. But was there perhaps another way of operating the service?

The inclusion of Whitechapel in Crossrail 1 makes this an important interchange station, since it will provide direct services to Maidenhead, Heathrow Airport, Shenfield and Abbey Wood, as well as the extended East London and the existing District and Hammersmith & City Underground services. It was then proposed that the East London Line services should be divided into two groups: one of eight-car trains for the longer-distance services, and the other of four cars for the core services.

The estimated capital cost was by then £1.3 billion, and the scheme met the Strategic Rail Authority's 'Value for Money' guidelines. It was assumed that the infrastructure controller and operator would be Network Rail. New trains would be required, and possibly a new franchise. This would be a high-density third rail operation by a main-line Train Operating Company, not London Underground.

In the event, matters proceeded rather differently, and with the abolition of the Strategic Rail Authority the East London Line project became funded by TfL's London Rail on 12 November 2004.

Above: Many of the DC lines stations have island platforms, but Harlesden has two side platforms. As can be seen here on 28 June 2008, the canopies are capacious, though a section of platform remains uncovered. John Glover

CHAPTER 11: **PASSENGER SERVICE DEVELOPMENT**

The railway has to cope with changing circumstances, even though possessing an infrastructure all the main components of which were laid down 150 or so years ago. This section considers the operation of the North London Line between North Woolwich or Broad Street and Richmond, the Gospel Oak-Barking and Clapham Junction spin-offs, and the Euston-Watford DC lines.

The service on these lines is described in terms of trains per hour. There are two principal periods on Mondays to Fridays: the peak hour and the rest. The direction used is that towards central London. While some services such as Richmond-Broad Street tended to operate at an even interval, this was nothing like as common in the earlier days. Variations had to be made to take account of other traffic and, latterly, the incidence of restrictions such as single-line sections.

The discussion starts with the situation in 1962. This was the scene against which Dr Beeching came to his conclusions and shows an operation seemingly in

good health. It must be pointed out that this sort of analysis can show only the trains that were being operated; it does not relate directly to the numbers of passengers being conveyed, though one hopes that there is some correlation. Clearly, long-term trends will be reflected in the service levels being provided, but that can be a very delayed reaction.

1962

So in 1962 the Richmond-Broad Street services provided a steady 4tph all day long, though this dropped to 2tph in the evenings. To this was added the peak-only operation from Watford Junction via Primrose Hill, which brought another 6tph into Broad Street. Trains from the Great Northern via Canonbury and from north of Watford Junction (there was still a locomotive-hauled service from Tring to Broad Street) are ignored for this purpose.

The Watford DC lines were busy, with 11 trains an hour, one of which originated from Croxley Green and

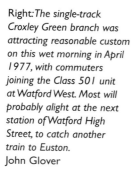

Right: The single-track Croxley Green branch was attracting reasonable custom on this wet morning in April 1977, with commuters joining the Class 501 unit at Watford West. Most will probably alight at the next station of Watford High Street, to catch another train to Euston.
John Glover

Above: A fair number of passengers at Broad Street await the arrival of this train from Richmond on 21 July 1980, but it is the evening peak in the City. The generally run-down appearance of the station by then can be seen, including the effects of the removal of about half of the overall roof. John Glover

Left: No 313108 pauses at Kensington Olympia in August 2003 with a service bound for Clapham Junction. By now a full-length platform has been restored to the eastern side of the station, albeit on the one and only southbound track. Reversible signalling does, however, allow all lines to be used in both directions. John Glover

another started from Bushey. But of those 11, only 5tph ended up at Euston. Thus for peak passengers Broad Street, serving the City, was as attractive as Euston for the West End. However, it is also necessary to take into account the Bakerloo, which in those days ran from Watford Junction occasionally and from Harrow & Wealdstone more frequently to Queen's Park, Oxford Circus and Elephant & Castle. Balancing the total service to be provided by what was then BR London Midland Region was always a headache.

Off-peak, the DC lines maintained a flat 3tph from Watford Junction to Euston. The vestiges of a middle-day Saturday peak for the 5½-day week were still apparent.

In the east, the Barking service originated from Kentish Town with no Gospel Oak connection. The service level was at 2tph all day, something that didn't change much over the years. On the Eastern Region, the service from North Woolwich ran to Stratford and sometimes to the then still open Palace Gates. This was for workers at 5tph in the peak, but only an irregular one of 2tph during the day.

1974

Moving on a decade to 1974, the peak service provision on the DC lines has eased considerably, with those to Broad Street halving and Euston not doing much better. This introduced the unusual feature of the peak service south of Willesden Junction, at 3tph, being less than the off-peak at 4tph. Essentially, the balance of demand during this period shifted from the City to the West End.

Similarly, the Richmond service was eased out to 3tph all day, though the morning peak showed the benefit of a Willesden Junction starter taking it up to 4tph over this section. There was a curious 4tph on summer Sundays only. Presumably this was the day that people went out to Hampstead Heath, Camden Road (for London Zoo), Kew Gardens or Richmond.

The Kentish Town-Barking service saw its off-peak service reduced to 1tph and the North Woolwich service, now running to Tottenham Hale only, reflected the drop of docklands employment.

PASSENGER SERVICE DEVELOPMENT

1984

By 1984 changes were beginning to happen. The DC lines operation was down again, slightly, although the service loss was to Euston rather than to Broad Street. The weekday off-peak Euston service was now 3tph, which it has maintained ever since. Some of the loss was perhaps due to the AC main-line electrification into Euston of 1966/67; where such trains stopped at stations served also by the DC services, they offered a more attractive service than hitherto.

Elsewhere, services from Richmond were 3tph at all times, daily, and what had become the Gospel Oak-Barking service regained its 2tph off-peak service. The biggest change was the introduction of a diesel service from Camden Road to North Woolwich, at a peak of

3tph and otherwise 2tph, although the service beyond Stratford was 2tph at all times.

1994

With the loss of Broad Street and electrification to North Woolwich, the Watford DC lines service was separated entirely from the North London service provision. This was now operated at 3tph without complications, all day on weekdays but 2tph on Sundays. It may be of interest to record the Croxley Green service as provided at this time. This is all that there was, and it would shortly become a taxi.

Elsewhere, what was temporarily the Richmond-Stratford service also operated at 4tph throughout (3tph Saturdays and 2tph Sundays). Services beyond

Above: At Harrow
& Wealdstone, Bakerloo
1972 Mk 2 trains meet
each other on 28 June 2008.
That approaching is just
entering service from the
turnback siding. Passengers
boarding Underground
trains here will experience
a distinct step down into
the vehicles. John Glover

Table 11.1 Mondays to Fridays

Watford Junction-Croxley Green. Service is
suspended on 30 May and 29 August

Miles		
0	Watford Junction	d 06 46
1	Watford High Street	d 06 48
2	Watford West	d 06 51
2¾	Croxley Green	a 06 55

Mondays to Fridays

Miles		
0	Croxley Green	d 06 59
¾	Watford West	d 07 01
1¾	Watford High Street	d 07 04
2¾	Watford Junction	a 07 07

NO SATURDAY OR SUNDAY SERVICE

Source: All System Passenger Timetable, Summer 1994

Clapham Junction and Kensington Olympia (only). By
1984 it had become a more generous 2tph peak-only
service, but it was now coming of age. There were still
only the three stations on the West London Line
mentioned in this paragraph, and all services were still
operated by the British Railways Board.

2004

The same service pattern operated on the Watford DC
lines, but the main service from Richmond once again
operated through to North Woolwich. This was at 4tph,
but only 2tph beyond Stratford due to the track singling
beyond Custom House station. One train working
beyond made a reliable 4tph frequency service impractical
over this stretch; while 3tph might have been achieved,
how could this be fitted into a 4tph service over the rest
of the line? Alternate trains were therefore terminated at
Stratford. Pressures of passenger numbers saw the peak
service elsewhere increased to 6tph for the section from
Camden Road to Stratford.

The Clapham Junction-Willesden Junction service
became 2tph all day, every day, by now with the
addition of West Brompton as a calling point. There
was another hourly longer-distance service to Milton
Keynes or Rugby, operated by South Central of the
Go-Ahead group, but not calling at Willesden Junction.
All other operations were by Silverlink Train Services,
a National Express company.

Operations at the present day are described later.

Stratford were suspended because of engineering
works in Silvertown Tunnel and elsewhere, and a bus
replacement operated. Somehow, longish-term service
interruptions seem to characterise this group of lines.

Newly introduced was a 2tph all-day service on the
West London Line between Clapham Junction and
Willesden Junction, but only on Mondays to Fridays.
This had existed earlier in vestigial form between

CHAPTER 12: **LONDON OVERGROUND**

Railways need to have a purpose and a role in the cities they serve, one of which is economic regeneration and another is social needs. But they are also the only effective way to transport large numbers of people to and from work in urban areas.

Thus in Docklands, 70,000 jobs were created between 1982 and 2005, while the rail market share to what is now Canary Wharf was a remarkable 91%. Rail has catered for all the growth, with road traffic remaining stagnant or even falling slightly.

Public transport trips have risen by 40%, three-quarters of which has been by rail. This has created severe capacity problems, and the situation is only going to get worse.

What can be done? Traffic by rail in the peaks is expected to grow by 30% in the next twenty years, with jobs concentrated in central London and Canary Wharf. Housing will remain distributed over a wide area, so public transport will have to provide the home-to-work links. Transport for London needs to develop services to meet future levels of demand and reduce overcrowding. In general, transport investment opens up access to jobs, education and leisure opportunities.

There are pragmatic ways of increasing capacity, such as more trains per hour, and more passengers per train. Tube-style rolling stock is perhaps the most effective way of packing more people in, though there are different sorts of requirements between inner and outer suburban operations.

Could spreading the peak help? This is going to have no more than a marginal effect; it is the sheer weight of numbers that has to be accommodated.

Then there is the contribution that could be made by an enhanced orbital rail network. On National Rail, the problems are line capacity, a routeing strategy for rail freight and operational conflicts where various services meet. Is there capacity to do all that might need to be done? Freight growth is also occurring, and the further expansion of East Coast ports could require many more train paths on a congested network.

Below: This is a geographic version of the map that shows the final form of the London Overground network when completed in 2012. It includes the full orbital network, together with its extensions. Courtesy of Transport for London

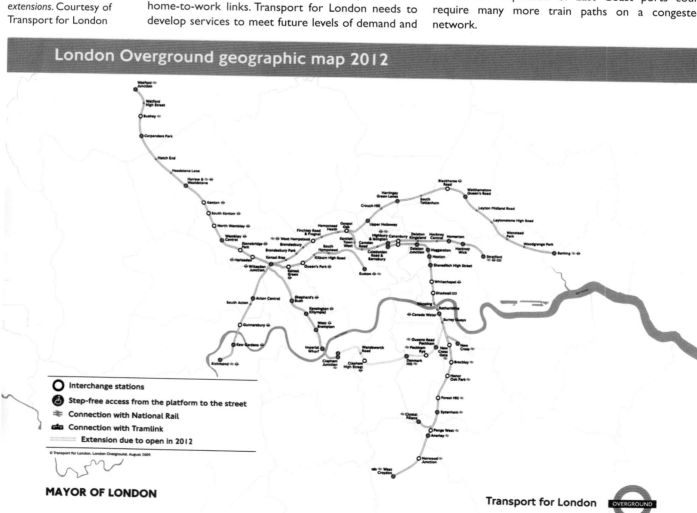

London Overground geographic map 2012

Interchange stations
Step-free access from the platform to the street
Connection with National Rail
Connection with Tramlink
Extension due to open in 2012

© Transport for London, London Overground, August 2009.

MAYOR OF LONDON

Transport for London OVERGROUND

London Rail

As a TfL subsidiary, London Rail deals with the National Rail network and has these main responsibilities:

* To oversee major new rail projects, including the £1 billion East London Line extension and the upgrade of London Overground
* To manage the London Rail Concession, which operates London Overground services
* To manage the operation of the Docklands Light Railway and that of Tramlink
* To support and develop Crossrail, as well as the Thameslink scheme
* To influence and support National Rail's contribution to an integrated public transport system for London
* To work with the Department for Transport and the rail industry to develop plans to accommodate London's future rail transport needs and to identify the best solutions for the rail network
* To liaise with the freight industry to support the sustainable movement of goods and the promotion of rail freight with respect to London's needs.

London Rail can also specify London's suburban rail services on certain routes outside the Greater London Authority boundary. This will enable future improvement and better co-ordination of the local rail services that serve London and its hinterland.

The London Overground brand and the TfL orange roundel were unveiled at City Hall on 5 September 2006.

On 14 February 2006, the then Mayor of London, Ken Livingstone, welcomed the transfer of responsibility for certain rail services from the government to Transport for London. From 11 November 2007, the North London Line, the Euston to Watford DC line, the West London Line and the Gospel Oak to Barking line were to be managed by Transport for London. Until then, the services would continue to be run by the then franchise holder, Silverlink (Metro), and funded by the Department for Transport. The date of transfer coincided with the expiry of the Silverlink franchise and the commencement of what was to become the London Overground concession, managed by Transport for London. Ownership of and responsibility for the infrastructure on these lines remained with Network Rail, no change from the then current situation.

Overground

In June 2007, London Overground Rail Operations Ltd (LOROL) was appointed to operate London Overground services, which started running on 11 November 2007. The concession runs for seven years from 11 November 2007 and a two-year extension is possible. The company is a 50/50 consortium of the Mass Transit Railway of Hong Kong and Deutsche Bahn Regio, which is now also the parent company of Chiltern Railways.

The concession (not a franchise) was let by Transport for London, and has been presented as a first step in relation to National Rail services around the capital generally. The routes are shown on the Underground diagram, and the intention is to offer a similar style of service frequency and quality.

The overall specification of the train and station services is the responsibility of TfL, including the requirements for quality standards, performance and facilities, and the funding of improvements to stations and the network. Track, signalling and infrastructure continue to be managed by Network Rail.

Above: The Silverlink livery applied here to No 313116 gives a cheerful touch to this December 2003 scene of the North Woolwich terminus, as the platform lights come on during the afternoon of a thoroughly wet day. John Glover

LONDON OVERGROUND

Above: *This is the new station at Imperial Wharf on the West London Line, seen here from street level on 12 April 2010 with a Southern train in the platforms above. As will be seen, the design is decidedly eye-catching; access is by lift or stairs.* John Glover

Right: *The new order of things at Willesden Junction: London Overground, National Rail and London Underground. There is none of the anonymity here that seems to be prevalent on some parts of the national network.* John Glover

LOROL is required to meet the overall specification of quality, safety, staffing, frequency and ticketing. As part of the initial changes, responsibility for the operation of 14 stations on the Overground network was transferred to London Underground Ltd. This was to reflect the situation where LUL was responsible for the major part of the stations' rail operations.

Unlike a National Rail franchisee, LOROL is not responsible for setting fares, procuring rolling stock or deciding service levels. These functions are retained by TfL, and there are similarities to the approach taken in the provision of London bus services.

The concession

London Overground operates more than 60km of route and serves 22 London boroughs directly, with 55 stations and 1,000 staff. The operating contract held by LOROL was valued at £100 million annually. There was an incentive system for good performance, with penalties for shortcomings, which included staff not being present, train cancellations, and delays for which the TOC could be held responsible. An additional 200 staff were taken on to ensure that all stations are manned at all times when they are open.

As the concession holder, LOROL thus has to concentrate on service provision to the specifications, quality and quantity demanded. In effect, it has to deliver the timetable, punctually and reliably, using trains that are clean and well presented. Passengers must be offered the standard of service that they might reasonably expect in terms of a welcoming travel environment, with staffed, clean and safe premises and trains. The staff are employed by LOROL.

TfL sets the fares levels and what is or is not accepted in terms of Railcards and concessionary travel. It monitors LOROL to ensure compliance with the terms and conditions of the contract, and the reduction of fares evasion is seen as important. There is a system of bonuses and penalties; the former come into play if the operator reaches significantly higher levels of performance and compliance than those specified in the contract, and correspondingly there are penalties for persistent failure to reach acceptable performance levels.

This is a gross cost concession, meaning that LOROL operates the concession at an agreed negotiated rate. It also collects the fares revenue, but this is handed over to TfL subject to a small revenue share. Demand growth has continued, to the extent that the revenue collected was up by nearly a fifth in the first year and continued to rise in the second, despite the recession.

The timetable operated is defined in the first instance by TfL, but in conjunction with LOROL and Network Rail. Thus, as in all such operations, the train service that it is desired to operate must have available paths in which to run the trains.

Infrastructure matters are the responsibility of Network Rail, apart from that on the former East London Line of London Underground and the new extensions, which are reserved to Transport for London; this includes

signalling and train control. Thus an additional interface has been created, which would not exist if the whole had become part of Network Rail's responsibility.

The goal

To secure a reasonably seamless transfer from one operator to another is one thing, but there was a lot more to be done. Much of this centred around the East London Line, and how that could be brought into a new orbital network. This is considered here under the following headings, which are addressed in turn.

* What was the potential for linking the East London Line to National Rail, both at the north end at (the original) Shoreditch, and at the two southern termini of New Cross and New Cross Gate?
* What were the demand projections in terms of the capacity required?
* If physical connections to National Rail were to be made at any or all of these, what should they aim to achieve and what service patterns should be operated?
* What physical works would be needed, on the East London Line itself, but also on those other parts of National Rail affected?
* How would matters such as rolling stock, depot provision and maintenance be achieved?
* What other upgrade works would be needed elsewhere on what was now London Overground?
* How would the whole be programmed?

It was intended that the London Overground services should be fully integrated into the TfL network and ticketing arrangements.

Initial routes

The initial routes of the London Overground network, collectively the North London Railway, and the concession now operated, were as follows:

* London Euston to Watford Junction (the DC local lines, 19 stations). From Queen's Park to Harrow & Wealdstone (10 stations) services are provided also by the Bakerloo Line of London Underground.
* Stratford to Richmond via Dalston Kingsland, Gospel Oak, Hampstead Heath and Willesden Junction (the North London Line, 23 stations). This is a joint operation with the District Line over the relatively short section between Gunnersbury and Richmond (three stations). Operation, by necessity, uses dual AC/DC multiple-units.
* Clapham Junction to Willesden Junction via Kensington Olympia (the West London Line, six stations). This line also requires dual AC/DC units and some services are extended eastwards to Stratford.
* Gospel Oak to Barking (12 stations). This line is not electrified.

For the time being, the operation of the East London Line of London Underground was excluded, pending

Above: *Honor Oak Park station buildings are on the road bridge that crosses the railway at that point, as seen here on 12 April 2010. Branding of the well-kept premises is noticeably absent, but London Overground operation here was still about six weeks away.* John Glover

Above: *Wanstead Park on the Tottenham & Hampstead sees No 170001 with a service for Barking on 19 August 2011. As on most of this line, the platforms are decidedly bare, but that is of little account on a fine day like this.* John Glover

its closure for substantial modification and modernisation. This included re-electrification at DC third rail and extensions at both ends. Operation of the network, as completed, is by LOROL.

While Network Rail remains the infrastructure controller of most of the network, control of the East London section itself between Dalston Junction and New Cross and the connections with the Southern network is exercised from the East London Line signalling control centre at New Cross Gate, which is owned by Transport for London.

North Woolwich closure

A further preliminary action was the closure of the five-mile North Woolwich branch from Stratford Low Level, with its intermediate stations at West Ham, Canning Town, Custom House and Silvertown. This was appearing increasingly as an anachronism, with progressive service cutbacks over the years. The gradual closure of the London Docks by the Port of London Authority and the dispersal of the workforce were largely responsible.

It then became a case of how to run the service most economically for the changing circumstances. The advent of third-rail electrification on 13 May 1985 in the heart of Great Eastern territory bordered on the bizarre, but it was a means to an end. Thus was established the through service between Richmond and North Woolwich, which would later be cut back to Stratford.

Initially, the trains used on it were the 2EPB sets from the Southern Region, and the whole did seem an

extremely unlikely combination on what was once a Great Eastern Railway branch serving London Docks. That the electrification should not have taken place until long after most of the workmen's traffic had disappeared was perhaps even odder.

The North Woolwich branch closed completely on 9 December 2006, after which the North London Line trains from Richmond terminated in the same Stratford platforms as used previously. The electrification of this branch thus lasted for 21½ years.

Stratford developments

As the two Stratford Low Level platforms were now required for the Docklands Light Railway extension from Canning Town, a new location had to be found for terminating North London Line trains. These are at a high-level site to the north of but adjacent to the main lines, with passenger access from the station subways. At the same time, 25kV AC electrification to these was installed, and the third rail was lifted at all points east of Dalston Kingsland. The platforms were built new and North London trains started using them on 24 April 2009. Thus ended any North London Line interests south of Stratford, but there was to be much more that would compensate for this loss.

In effect, the whole area was instead colonised by other railways. Thus the Jubilee Line extension of London Underground (Canning Town, West Ham and Stratford) opened in 1999. The Docklands Light Railway, which already served Canning Town and Custom House, had in effect also scooped the traffic

from Silvertown and North Woolwich with its stations on the Woolwich Arsenal extension at London City Airport and King George V (2005). It was then set to make a further extension from Canning Town to Stratford International, as far as Stratford over the trackbed of the former Great Eastern branch (2011).

Orbital working

The completion of work on the South London Line in 2012 results in a new orbital rail line around London. Thus it will be possible to travel between any two points on the direct route with a maximum of one change of train. Journeys that also involve the radial lines incorporated into the London Overground network may need a second change, but the aim of a simplified network will be achieved.

The fact that such journeys will be possible does not necessarily mean that they will be the fastest means of getting between two given points. Highbury & Islington to West Brompton, for instance, may be quicker using the Victoria and District lines, rather than catching an Overground train via Willesden Junction. On the other hand, how many people want to make journeys of that sort of length when neither is in a location that might be termed central London? Urban railways of this nature are more likely to get the

Above: *A smartly turned out Hatch End, with No 313113 arriving on 15 April 2010. This station is well equipped, never having been 'modernised' other than in the sense of having ticket entry gates provided and similar.* John Glover

Left: *Above the entrance to Hatch End station is this remarkable coat of arms of the then owning company, the London & North Western Railway, complete with clock and weathervane above on the roof. Quite what inspired the LNWR to provide such a showpiece station is unclear, but the results are outstanding to this day. The date is 15 April 2010.* John Glover

Right: *A pair of Class 378 trains stands in the centre two platforms at the newly created underground (!) Dalston Junction station, which is very different from its predecessor. It is 28 April 2010, the first full day of public service, and trains are going no further than New Cross or New Cross Gate.* John Glover

Opposite: *The City beckons, though No 378146 will get no nearer than Shoreditch High Street, the next station. To reach that it will, perhaps unexpectedly, turn sharp left. This is the view from Hoxton station platforms of the departing train on 28 April 2010.* John Glover

bulk of their patronage from short-distance passengers. Linking the services so that the need for change of train is minimised is more a convenience for some rather than the many. It also makes for economical service operation, since driver and train keep going rather than stopping to reverse the train with the driver changing ends.

Why not then run at least some of the services around a notional circle, on a continuous basis? The problem associated with this approach is that it is very difficult to regulate the services adequately. If things started to run late, how would it be corrected if there was no standing time anywhere, or perhaps no locations at which to stand? What would then happen to the punctuality of other services that used the same routes, even if only in part? A secondary reason is that the effects of incidents of perhaps a more serious nature are transmitted throughout the system, rather than being confined to discrete sections of line. Readers will be aware that since December 2009 London Underground's Circle Line no longer performs a true circular operation for these sorts of reasons.

To some, orbital services suggest a railway that goes from nowhere to nowhere, with patronage to match. They are thus of limited importance. Others will point out that they fill a useful gap in the transport system of the capital between the radial routes of both the Underground and National Rail. They are also free of road congestion, though this doesn't mean free of all interruptions to service.

Transfer from Silverlink

What were previously Silverlink Metro services form what might now be described as the northern and western arms of London Overground. Silverlink Metro was operated by the same company, National Express, as Silverlink County. However, one was an electrified 25kV AC network, while the other had its roots in the

traditional DC operation. Both had a small amount of diesel operation.

Thus there was little in common between the two, which perhaps made it easier to separate them. It would appear that the split had the classic effect, with the then franchisee losing interest in the services concerned. If a company is going to lose the services anyway, either because it decides not to bid or in the event is unsuccessful, there is little incentive to do any more than is absolutely necessary for the remainder of the franchise period.

Maybe this had been going on for rather longer. In October 2008, TfL felt able to describe the stations it had taken over in the following terms. 'Decades of neglect and under-investment had resulted in many stations becoming dingy, dirty and inefficient. So we gave all our stations a thorough "deep clean"... We scraped away the layers of chewing gum and grime that had been allowed to accumulate over the years, we repaired broken fittings and equipment, we installed new bench-style customer seating and we smartened the walls up by giving them a fresh coat of paint.'

Were the stations really that bad?

The rolling stock was similarly derided. 'Old-fashioned, neglected trains [that] were completely out of step with our ambition to provide an excellent service for our customers. Rather than making a series of superficial improvements ... we have invested more than £260 million in commissioning an impressive fleet of new vehicles that have been especially designed to meet the needs of London Overground passengers...' and so on.

One must allow for a degree of copywriter's licence. Outgoing administrations, especially political ones, are often denounced by their successors in terms of this nature.

And the Class 313s? They have been spruced up and are now providing further service along the South Coast for Southern.

CHAPTER 13: **UPGRADING AND EXTENSIONS**

Above: A heavy train of perhaps limestone passes in a southerly direction through Kensington Olympia behind EWS No 66218 in August 2003. Freight trains when full, like this one, take some stopping, and if they do have to stop it takes some time to get back up to speed. Thus the aim is to keep them moving whenever possible, however slowly. John Glover

Work at the stations inherited by London Overground (or sometimes London Underground) was divided into four phases, as follows.

Phase 1 concerned the installation of gating at the more important stations, and the acceptance of the Oyster ticketing system for pay-as-you-go travel. (It had only been accepted previously when the Oyster card had a Travelcard embedded in it.) These were early concerns, and much of the programme was completed by the time of the station operator changeover. This was the first time for around forty years that all stations would be staffed during opening hours.

Phase 2 was to clean and repair the premises as necessary, and this was completed by the summer of 2008. It should be noted that this was all it was, and what one might have expected to be part of a company's running costs.

It was then supplemented by Phase 3, major refurbishment works, which had to meet the requirements of all the stakeholders, including Network Rail. Some of this was expensive work, such as the installation of help points and the associated cabling. Work started at five stations and it is intended that all will be complete by the time of the London Olympic Games in 2012.

Perhaps one of the most important objectives in terms of attracting new patronage and retaining the existing was to try and get rid of that pervasive feeling of urban decay. This makes too many stations feel unattractive, even if they are reasonably well swept, clean and clear of graffiti. Many of them seemed to belong to another era which had little to do with the present.

Station remodelling

Then we come to Phase 4, which includes perhaps extensive remodelling at certain locations. Thus Hackney Central is about 100 metres from the south end of the platforms of Hackney Downs on the Great Eastern's Enfield and Chingford lines, which cross the North London at right angles on an overbridge. Could a better interchange be achieved, given also that there is an inconvenient road in the way?

Similarly, at West Hampstead there are long-standing plans to link the North London Line station directly with the Jubilee Line station on the other side of West End Lane. This has the Chiltern Line adjacent to it, presently without platforms, and also West Hampstead Thameslink, a little to the north. The whole would offer very considerable interchange possibilities, but it is a major project in all senses.

Gospel Oak is an interesting location, which is also a possibility for reconstruction. At present the North London Line has side platforms at high level connected by a subway, which also leads to the station exit. On the north side, the eastbound North London platform links to a single terminal platform for the diesel services from Barking. Beyond that there is a pair of lines at present used only for freight between the Tottenham & Hampstead, the North London and Willesden. If the Gospel Oak-Barking line was to be electrified, ways would have to be found to provide platforms at Gospel Oak on the through lines. The alternative, using the present layout, would be for trains from (say) Clapham Junction to Barking to miss out a call at Gospel Oak altogether. Would the terminating platform still be needed? It would remain a useful facility to reverse trains short of the main line, and as a general aid to operational flexibility and hence service reliability.

New brooms

This was the prelude to what became a large-scale investment plan to produce a new Metro-style railway, and perhaps represented a softening up of the passengers for the major disruption that this would later cause. But there were other problems.

As TfL found in the first year or so after the 2007 handover, ticket irregularities were running at about 15%. Actions taken meant that this dropped to 2%. This was helped by the acceptance of Oyster and the installation of ticket gates at some, but not all, stations. Oyster payment was accepted for all pay-as-you-go fares from 11 September 2009. All stations are now staffed at all times that trains are running.

The Passenger Performance Measurement (PPM), which affects all National Rail operators, took what is now LOROL from among the least well performing operations to a place in the top five. The PPM measures items such as service punctuality and reliability, and was a moving annual average of 95.2% in mid-2011.

Passenger concerns about the service and related matters as measured by the National Passenger Survey using 'mystery shoppers' brought the company from 57% to 75%. However, the massive rebuilding programme, discussed elsewhere, has meant extended periods of complete service suspension on the North London Line east of Gospel Oak, measured in months rather than days. Thus there wasn't anything for passengers to complain about apart from the replacement bus services, where operated, but it was also unlikely to earn many passenger plaudits.

South of the river

South of the river matters were more straightforward. The Southern Railway franchise is operated by the Go-Ahead company, which was also the operator of the core of the previous franchise. The new franchise

Below: *The two systems of the North London Line and the Watford DC are linked at Willesden, where a spur joins the line from Kensal Rise to the DC line facing north. It may be seen to the extreme left of this picture of a 1972 Mk 2 train leaving Willesden Junction for Queen's Park and Elephant & Castle on 14 April 1994. John Glover*

Above: *Crouch Hill station
on the Tottenham &
Hampstead line has, like
other London Overground
stations, been provided with
staffed accommodation. The
ticket office here sits rather
uncomfortably to the right
of the steps leading to the
far platform (towards
Barking). But there is little
in the way of alternatives;
the bridge carries a road,
and its use as a railway
footbridge is purely incidental.
The date is 12 September
2009.* John Glover

Right: *Camden Road
Junction signalbox, seen here
on 12 September 2009,
stands at an important pinch
point, where services from
Dalston on two sets of tracks
for most of the way diverge
towards Primrose Hill (left)
and Gospel Oak (right).
Note too the complexities
of what needs to be done in
terms of electrical supplies.*
John Glover

Electric trains for
branch line raise
pantograph before
proceeding

313
UNITS
PAN
UP

started on 20 September 2009, with the future loss of the local services on the line to London Bridge and later the South London Line already known about and factored into the equation.

In practice, what happened was that the stations on the lines from West Croydon and Crystal Palace were transferred to London Overground on 25 September 2009. A full list of the stations presently served or to be served by London Overground, and the station operators, appears as Appendix A.

New routes

Given that the existing routes north and west of the capital had in many ways almost defined themselves, what else was needed to complete an orbital route? In many ways, this had been considered before, and has been discussed in the preceding pages. In all cases, earlier attempts at orbital operations seem to have failed on the basis that the routes they offered were often too circuitous. This was not necessarily a problem in itself, but the journey times that resulted made them thoroughly uncompetitive.

The competition in this instance was not so much other main-line railways, but the developing networks of motor buses and roads, then what became the Underground network, assisted by that crowd-consumer, the electric tram. This last was cheap to operate, gave cheap fares in return, and its rates of acceleration coupled with high service frequency made it difficult to beat.

Railway electrification activity was DC with a mixture of third and fourth rail with the exception of the AC overhead Brighton line. This was especially strong in the Edwardian era of the early 20th century.

Demand

How well would passengers respond to a revamped and revitalised railway network? It was important not to repeat earlier mistakes, though one major factor had intervened that was to help the railway: road congestion. Thus the speed of buses on roads, the trams having long departed, was not likely to be the cause of the siphoning off of traffic.

The lack of a coherent railway network outside the Underground was also a possible reason. Where activities are largely radial in nature, the links between them are of secondary importance, and this has already been discussed. Variations of ownership in the different lines involved did not make any form of unification easy, and there was perhaps general expectation that

this was in any event not a major railway activity. The conclusion of Dr Beeching that railways of this nature were largely superfluous has already been mentioned, but that was half a century ago.

Overall, it was felt that the bare bones of an orbital network were in place, and indeed this had been the case for many years. These needed to be linked up properly with other TfL services, and service frequencies would also have to be enhanced to provide a real benefit to users.

Thus it was concluded that there was a good case for the investment of a considerable amount of resources and initiating the operation of a service that would be much superior to that which had been available hitherto.

It was predicted that, in 2011, 33 million people will have used the new East London route, equating to around 100,000 per day, and demand is forecast to increase to 40 million by 2016, a growth of around one-fifth. The former East London Underground line prior to its closure carried many fewer, at about nine million passengers every year, or 30,000 a day.

New objectives, north

The major opportunities revolved around the East London Line. If this was to be extended from Shoreditch at the northern end, where might it go? And although both the southern branches to New Cross and New Cross Gate terminated in bay platforms of the Network Rail stations of the same name, was extension either worthwhile or feasible?

It was concluded early on that as only the Great Eastern main line to Liverpool Street lay beyond the Shoreditch East London station, there was little that might be achieved in that direction. But there was another possibility, which involved the former Broad Street North

London line stub from Dalston Junction. In 1985 London Underground had proposed to connect the East London Line to the North London Line viaduct and run to Dalston Junction only, but no funding was available.

The East London Line extension was transferred from being a Strategic Rail Authority project to TfL. Broad Street station itself had disappeared into the 1990s Broadgate commercial development, but most of the viaduct on which the two miles of track was laid remained in existence. Some of the bridges had been removed and the viaduct itself was in what might be termed a variable condition, but there was at least a possibility here. Could the two be joined, thus creating a new route north from Whitechapel via Shoreditch to Dalston? What communities could be served in the process?

The answer was positive, and the scheme that was adopted is described later.

Other traffic

Another defined requirement, albeit short-term, was to facilitate access to Stratford for the London Games in 2012. This required, above all else, available line capacity. For this, resignalling was the key, to shorten the lengths of block sections and to recognise the inherent difficulties of moving long and heavy freight trains over the same tracks as a reasonably frequent local passenger service without causing delays to either.

This is quite a tall order, given that there would be no passing loops over the five miles from west of Highbury & Islington to the approaches to Stratford. In this section, local trains at quarter-hourly intervals would also be making six station stops. There are similarly no loops between Camden Road and Willesden Junction on the route via Hampstead Heath. This is another six miles, with eight stations.

Right: This is Caledonian Road station on an unknown date, but when it still had four platforms and the station entrance was at the eastern end. G. Freeman Allen's generalised description seems to fit well: 'Nobody could claim the gloomy, smoke-blackened North London stations as among the glories of British station architecture, but their drab buildings and offices seem to have been laid out on spacious lines.' Author's collection

Similar situations arise elsewhere on the Overground network, notably on the West London Line. They are a basic operational problem when running a multi-purpose railway like the national system. Yes, one traffic might in theory give way to another, but what then becomes of it? Shifting the problem elsewhere in a geographical sense by rerouteing trains might help the local situation at the points of conflict. However, if this is achieved only at the expense of disruptive effects elsewhere, it is at best only a partial solution. With the rail traffic growth of the last decade or so, track capacity has proved to be a very valuable commodity. If there isn't enough of it at the times and places that it is wanted, someone will suffer.

It was also desirable to continue to provide for other miscellaneous train movements, such as the short-lived open access operation by the Anglia Train Operating Company (TOC) between the Great Eastern main line and Basingstoke, or stock movements to and from the Great Northern via the Canonbury spur. The latter is retained, but with a link towards Stratford only.

Platform extension

Other essential work was to extend platforms so that four cars could be accommodated at all stations. While all the North London stations from Broad Street to Watford Junction and Richmond (now in effect from Canonbury) were able to take six cars of the Class 501 stock built in 1957 with a total length of about 111 metres, subsequent rationalisation saw many of the platforms reduced to all that was needed for three cars of Class 313 stock (61 metres). This work varied in complexity according to location, one of the most difficult of which was at Willesden Junction High Level. Here, the platform formed part of the bridge over the DC lines, and when the bridge was last renewed the opportunity had been taken to reduce its width on the grounds that this part of the platform was no longer required. The other end of the platform abuts the bridge over the West Coast Main Line, so extension there was no answer.

Resignalling was needed to permit an increase in train service frequency and also to accommodate the changes described in the track layout. There was also a general requirement to renew and upgrade the track and other infrastructure as required.

Cost

The cost of the extensive works was £326 million, which was shared by TfL, the Olympic Delivery Authority, Network Rail and the Department for Transport. The broad aim was to double the line's capacity. The works were delivered by Network Rail and Carillion.

Above: *No 66717 heads a freight west through Harringay Green Lanes on 13 April 2010. The use of the Tottenham & Hampstead line whenever possible was all but obligatory while widespread engineering work had closed the North London west of Stratford.* John Glover

CHAPTER 14: **BUILDING THE NEW EAST LONDON**

The construction work to be undertaken on the extended East London Line, now the East London Railway, is considered here.

Preparatory work

Preparatory work for the new East London Railway from Dalston Junction southwards started in June 2005 and was completed by the end of 2006. Carried out by Taylor Woodrow, the work involved replacing and refurbishing 22 bridges along the disused Kingsland Viaduct. The main construction work consisted of:

* replacement of approximately 7.4km of track and signalling equipment on the existing East London Line to convert it to National Rail operating standards
* installation of approximately 3.6km of new track and signalling on the northern extension from Whitechapel to Dalston Junction
* construction of four new stations with step-free access at Dalston Junction, Haggerston, Hoxton and Shoreditch High Street

* construction of a railway flyover just north of New Cross Gate station to connect the up local line from West Croydon to the northbound East London just short of Canal Junction (where the New Cross line diverges)
* construction of a new maintenance depot and stabling area at New Cross Gate.

This work required the closure of the Underground East London Line in its entirety from 22 December 2007 until 27 April 2010.

The scheme was eventually broken into three phases, linked to when they were authorised:

* Phase 1: Dalston Junction to New Cross, Crystal Palace and West Croydon
* Phase 1a: Highbury & Islington to Dalston Junction
* Phase 2: Surrey Quays to Clapham Junction

It will be noted that this refers almost entirely to the East and South London DC-only lines. Extensive work was to take place also on the North London Line under the auspices of Network Rail to accommodate

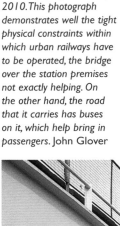

Below: No 378135 arrives at Surrey Quays on 28 April 2010. This photograph demonstrates well the tight physical constraints within which urban railways have to be operated, the bridge over the station premises not exactly helping. On the other hand, the road that it carries has buses on it, which help bring in passengers. John Glover

Left: *This major bridge over Kingsland Road to the south of Hoxton station survived to be reused in the service restoration along most of the Broad Street viaduct. It was photographed on 28 April 2010.* John Glover

Left: *Shoreditch High Street station entrance, seen here on 28 April 2010, looks as if it has been built to be incorporated into an office block or similar, which for some reason the builders forgot to construct. Together with the platforms above street level, that is more or less what it is hoped will happen. The railway has brought the means of getting to the area by train, and land use and land values are likely to reflect that.* John Glover

freight traffic in particular, but only modest attention would be given to the West London and virtually none at all to the DC Watford lines.

Whitechapel to Shoreditch

Since the existing Shoreditch station had no potential for line extension, it would need to be closed and the approach to it diverted. Closure took place in 2006, and London Underground services no longer proceeded north of Whitechapel.

The East London platforms at the latter are in a cutting, and the immediate need was to construct a ramp north from Whitechapel station to bring the lines to the surface and at a sufficient elevation to cross the Great Eastern lines into Liverpool Street on a new bridge, GE19. They would then proceed on a new viaduct to the elevated Shoreditch High Street station.

The new bridge was fabricated on land beside the railway and was later slid into position. This decision was based on land availability and the wish to minimise

Above: *Haggerston station is a modern design, which does not rely on the old viaduct for the entrance to the premises. It comes the closest of the new stations to making a visual statement of itself; people who do not know might well ask, 'What's that building?'* John Glover

disruption to the existing train services, but it involved a most unfortunate incident. The new bridge was to have an 84-metre span and needed to be 10.4 metres wide to carry a double-track railway, which was to cross the Great Eastern at an oblique angle. In order to join the two parts of the East London, it was also to be on a substantial gradient of 1 in 30, or 3.3%, rising from east to west. Consequently there was a difference of 2.75 metres in the height of the support abutments on each side.

Prefabrication complete, this massive bridge structure was launched into position over the Bank Holiday weekend of 3-5 March 2008. The equipment used for the launch was then dismantled over the succeeding weeks and removed, but work on lowering the bridge into its final position had not been completed.

On 28 May 2008, the temporary supports that were being used to support the bridge failed at about 19:16, causing the partly completed deck of the bridge

to drop by 200mm at the eastern end, which sent shock waves through the entire structure. This resulted in concrete planks being displaced and falling from the deck onto the tracks below.

The 19:17 train from Liverpool Street to Southend Victoria then hit some of the debris, following which all trains were halted. Fortunately there were no casualties, and damage to equipment was only superficial. Nevertheless, electrical isolations meant that around 1,000 passengers had to be walked from the ten trains affected, and the line did not reopen until 09:30 the following morning, after stabilising work on the bridge had been undertaken.

The report issued by the Rail Accidents Investigation Board cited a number of causes, direct and indirect, and made recommendations. Essentially, the cause was inadequate planning and lack of design in the bridge repositioning, unauthorised modifications and other civil engineering shortcomings.

Shoreditch to Hoxton

The railway, by now facing west, reaches the area once dominated by the Bishopsgate Goods Depot, which was destroyed by fire in December 1964 and billed at the time as the most costly disaster in railway history. This is the site of the new Shoreditch High Street station, which is elevated above ground level prior to crossing Shoreditch High Street itself on an elegant new bowstring bridge weighing 350 tonnes and 35 metres long. The railway then continues to swing north to join the old formation from Broad Street.

Shoreditch High Street station presents a curious appearance, in that it has been designed so that it can be incorporated into a future commercial development. The exterior can only be described as an unfinished box-like structure, and it is almost completely windowless. Entering it in broad daylight at ground level, it is rather disconcerting to find on reaching the two side platforms above that illumination is entirely by artificial light. The station is judged sufficiently 'underground' for it to be subject to the s12 fire regulations.

Daylight can indeed be seen at the end of one of the artificial 'tunnels', but it is blocked at the other due to the line curvature.

Despite immediate appearances, the location of the new station is a mere 500 metres from the City, and thus within reasonable walking distance. It thus has the potential to become an integral part of the City, rather than the site of a disused yard.

Once on the old route, the railway recrosses what is now the southern end of Kingsland Road – using a surviving girder bridge – shortly before reaching the new station site of Hoxton. This is a quiet back-street location that is not easy to find for the uninitiated, though the location is basically good. The entrance leads to a ticket hall area beneath the viaduct, from which steps or lifts take passengers up to the two side platforms. A similar arrangement may be found at the other new stations. At platform level there is no

mistaking that this is in the open air, and long side walls provide some shelter here and also at nearby Haggerston.

Hoxton is the bulk electricity supply point for the East London section. Power is taken from the National Grid at 132kV and is then transformed and rectified to 750V DC using 33kV switchgear in the substation.

Hoxton to Dalston Junction

On leaving Hoxton the line soon passes over a new bowstring bridge across the Regent's Canal and a minor road. The previous removal of this bridge had allowed road vehicle height restrictions to be abolished, so how was its reinstatement to be handled?

This was solved quite simply. To put the new bridge in place, the road had to be closed for a period anyway. The local authority took careful note of any problems, which didn't seem to be too many. When all was finished, the hoardings were removed, bollards were put in the road and, with the necessary orders made, the road closure became permanent. The Regent's Canal bridge has two spans, each 10 metres high and 48 metres long, and was the first bowstring girder bridge on a railway in Britain.

The new line continues on the former viaduct to the site for the third new station, generally similar to Hoxton, at Haggerston. This is an area with mixed types of dwellings; the response of one group of residents on being told that a new station was being planned was an objection on the grounds that 'this is a residential area'. Others might consider this a very positive contribution to local amenities, not least in its likely effects on house values.

Passenger access at both Haggerston and Hoxton stations is through the existing arches, and the ability to build the station platforms was helped greatly by the former quadruple-track status of the railway.

The railway then descends gradually to ground level, which was useful in terms of providing construction access to the line generally. The downward slope continues to a completely new Dalston Junction station, located in an area where much housing development is under way. The London Development Authority has provided some funding to kick-start such schemes, and Dalston Junction is to become a major centre. The station has been built on a very thick concrete raft to support development above. There is also a bus station.

Investment in transport infrastructure is seen as essential for growth and to support the economy.

Dalston Junction to Highbury & Islington

Should Dalston Junction be the final terminus? One snag was its distance of about 200 metres from Dalston Kingsland station on the North London Line to Stratford, which didn't exactly aid interchange between the two. It was also felt that Highbury & Islington station, a mile and a half west, would be a better terminus as it provided interchange with both the Victoria Line of London Underground and the Moorgate/Welwyn Garden City/Hertford North service of First Capital Connect. It would also serve the existing intermediate station of Canonbury, which could act as a more satisfactory interchange for those proceeding from south of Dalston Junction to east of Dalston Kingsland. In the event, Dalston Junction was built with four platforms: two centre terminating roads and two through lines.

The two outer tracks continue in a sharp westward curve, to align them with the North London tracks, which themselves have been shifted to the north. Fortunately, the whole formation from this point west to Camden Road Junction formerly carried four tracks, which made at least partial reinstatement easier.

Above: This 28 April 2010 view is from Haggerston towards Dalston Junction, just visible in the distance, and an area that includes that of the former main construction base. In the course of that short distance, the railway descends from above to below street level. John Glover

Above: *At platform level, Shadwell was not the most enticing of stations. At the northern end, seen here on 26 April 2006, daylight does penetrate, though it also reveals the substantial extra help needed to keep the tunnel walls the correct distance apart and prevent them from imploding.* John Glover

Third rail

These tracks, electrified as third rail DC only, are for the exclusive use of the East London Line trains and continue to run parallel with the North London (25kV AC) through Canonbury to where they end at Highbury & Islington. Other traffic, freight as well as North London passenger trains, uses the reinstated tracks on the north side.

At Highbury there is a single-line connection between the two sets of tracks, one pair DC and the other AC, but this is for stock movement purposes only. Another possible connection, but with passive provision only, is from Dalston Junction eastwards towards Stratford. Use of this would require dual AC/DC-fitted Class 378/2 units, which are not at present seen on the DC-only East London and Southern section of London Overground.

The eventual result was that Phase 1 of the northern extension was commissioned on 27 April 2010, and Phase 1a, which took it to Highbury, on 28 February 2011.

It may be noted that it was possible to complete the whole of the works between Dalston and Whitechapel on a formation that did not have to carry other rail traffic at any time. Contractors could thus have a complete and permanent possession. There were of course many other interfaces, particularly with highway authorities, which posed their own problems, but keeping the railway going in the interim was not an issue.

The enabling works were undertaken by Taylor Woodrow in a £30 million contract that involved replacing or refurbishing all the bridges along the disused structures on the Broad Street section.

Whitechapel to New Cross and New Cross Gate

London Underground relinquished the operation of the East London Line and the last trains ran on 22 December 2007. From then until 27 April 2010 it was closed for all traffic purposes. Replacement bus services were run for the most part, but this did not include a means of getting over the Thames between Wapping and Rotherhithe. For this, users were advised to use the Jubilee Line at Canada Water to reach the north bank at Canary Wharf, and bus connections as necessary.

The four stations at Shadwell, Wapping, Rotherhithe and Canada Water are underground, to the extent that very little daylight penetrates to the platforms. Whitechapel platforms, where a new linking footbridge was constructed, are in more or less open cutting, and the same could be said of Surrey Quays.

Right: *The surface buildings at Shadwell East London Line station in Cable Street were rebuilt in 1983, with the distinctive results shown in this 2006 view. Unfortunately, as it was to turn out, they weren't really in the right place. This led to substantial reconstruction during the subsequent line closure, which was mostly aimed at conversion of the line to National Rail standards.* John Glover

Access works, including the provision of additional emergency exits, took place, and Shadwell underwent a considerable reconstruction of the ticket hall area. This was the result of an unfortunate station reconstruction in the 1970s, when the new building was placed some distance away from what would later become the staircase access to the Docklands Light Railway station of the same name. This has now been corrected by providing a second exit at the other (north) end.

Slab track has been used throughout the tunnel sections, which helps to provide additional vertical clearances to suit full-sized rolling stock. The whole was also resignalled, now controlled from the new facility at New Cross Gate, and third rail took the place of fourth rail electrification.

Tunnel dimensions

The tunnel dimensions at Wapping and Rotherhithe are so tight that the 'next train' indicators have had to be placed partly over the tracks, rather than wholly over the platforms. One problem had been the unsuitability of Wapping and Rotherhithe stations to take longer trains due to platform dimensions and access restrictions. In November 2002, the SRA had confirmed closure proposals, although they were reprieved by the Mayor in 2004 under the Phase 1 proposal.

New Cross termini

There are double termini at the southern end of the line beyond Surrey Quays, at New Cross and New Cross Gate, serving Southeastern and Southern Railway routes respectively, and passengers interchanging to and from them. The stations are in reality no more than 600 metres apart along the A2, New Cross Road, which runs directly between them. However, from the point of view of East London passengers who want to continue by National Rail services, the ability to access both stations directly is a very useful facility.

The line to New Cross continues as previously, with cross-platform connections to Southeastern services.

The line to New Cross Gate has been doubled throughout, with a new single-track flyover built across the Network Rail lines between London Bridge and New Cross Gate. This is to enable London Overground up trains from Croydon to reach the East London line without conflict, and is an essential ingredient in being able to provide a service of 8tph. The flyover was moved into position on 10 May 2008, and crosses the rail access to the four-road heavy maintenance shed as well as the Network Rail lines used by rail services to London Bridge.

The former terminating bay on the down side of New Cross Gate station has been extended so that it now provides a direct link to the Network Rail down slow line.

Above: *This is the main entrance to Shadwell station today, as reconstructed during the recent closure. Photographed on 28 April 2010, it has noticeably changed its character from that built in 1983, and now of course carries London Overground branding.* John Glover

Left: *This is the new 'other' entrance to Shadwell station, a ticket hall distance away but otherwise immediately behind the existing one. This will be much more convenient for passengers wishing to change to or from the Docklands Light Railway.* John Glover

New depot and control centre

Required in the vicinity of New Cross Gate was a new depot for the Class 378 trains. This replaced the outmoded and much too small East London depot at New Cross and was intended to provide complete maintenance facilities. Most of the depot is situated between the down East London Line and the down slow National Rail tracks.

New Cross Gate depot opened in March 2010. It consists of a reversible entry/exit track to the East London in both directions, a washer road, eight berthing sidings, four of which are double-ended, a wheel lathe road and a heavy cleaning road. There is a section of 25kV AC track at New Cross Gate depot for overhead line testing of AC units.

Right: *Slab track has been a feature of a lot of the new work and can be seen here at Surrey Quays with No 378142 arriving with a service for Dalston Junction on 28 April 2010. No, it doesn't have any tendency to creep over time like ballasted track, but you do need to be certain that where you put it is where you are going to want it in the future. Moving it is a major matter. John Glover*

Also within the depot premises is the Operational Building Complex. This has three floors, containing the drivers' signing on and off point, general staff facilities, offices and on the top floor the East London Line control room. This oversees train operations, station operation and security, together with fault reporting. Facilities include the CCTV monitors and the signalling displays which cover the tracks between the Dalston Junction and New Cross Gate areas, where they interface with the Network Rail signalling centres at Upminster and London Bridge respectively. The only part of the East London managed by TfL is that which was formerly part of London Underground, that is to New Cross and the junction with Network Rail at New Cross Gate, plus the new section north of Whitechapel to Shoreditch High Street and thence over the viaduct to a little beyond the Dalston Junction station area. Beyond both of these, Network Rail takes over in what might be called 'the normal manner'.

The workshop building contains four maintenance tracks. Three of these are for general maintenance, which is carried out on a mileage-based interval system, rather than elapsed time. These are equipped with pits, walkways and roof access gantries. The latter are used to maintain the roof-mounted air-conditioning equipment, but could also be used to maintain the overhead equipment from the dual voltage sets if required. The fourth road is equipped for jacking and can lift an entire 4-car train simultaneously.

The maintenance facility at Willesden, as used formerly by Silverlink, remains in use.

New Cross Gate to Crystal Palace

While the New Cross stub (the last section to the terminus is single-track) remained as it was, great things were proposed for the western arm terminating at New Cross Gate. Through running to the four-track railway from London Bridge to Windmill Bridge, Croydon, and beyond was clearly a possibility, but this would add another radial service. In this it would be broadly akin to the Watford DC lines service in the north. Such an extension, whatever its merits, would not have any effect on the provision of an orbital service. The further possibilities for that are considered later.

The decision regarding the southern route was to provide services of equal frequencies to West Croydon and to Crystal Palace. Works included the gating of all stations, with Crystal Palace station restored to showpiece standard. This is a Grade I listed building,

Below: *The delightful murals at Wapping, showing scenes past, have survived into the present era; this photograph was taken on 18 April 1998. John Glover*

and the original ticket office on the bridge is being restored to take the place of the 1970s glass structure that has been used since then. Until now, entry from the street has involved descending by umpteen stairs to a sort of mezzanine level. From here one continued down another set of stairs to the lines to Norwood Junction (not TfL), or to those from London Bridge. Or it is up more stairs, over a bridge, and down to the far platform for trains to London Bridge.

The scheme is costing £8 million and is part funded as a joint Railway Heritage Trust, National Rail Improvement Programme, TfL and DfT's Access for All initiative.

Also required at Crystal Palace was the creation of two additional terminal platforms on the Sydenham side of the station and the provision of suitable access from the station footbridge. This spans what until recently were the only two tracks to remain.

West Croydon

Some modest works have been undertaken at West Croydon, such as filling in the bay, once Platform 2. This was used formerly by the Wimbledon service, which is now part of London Tramlink. One odd result is that the canopy still follows the old platform alignments, but for no apparent reason.

The pre-existing terminal bay, Platform 1, is still available for reversing trains. A second means is via a new centrally placed turnback siding provided beyond the ends of the two side platforms. This allows trains to arrive in Platform 4 (towards Sutton) and discharge their passengers, proceed to the turnback and reverse to return from Platform 2. As this was already possible, few other changes have been needed to prepare it for its new role.

Otherwise, the substitution of a set of trains of one operator for those of another on an operating electrified railway is not a major matter on today's National Rail network, which has grown used to occasional changes in franchise operator. It has affected branding and ticketing matters, together with other changes related to the intended service revisions by the new incumbent.

Above: *The East London terminal platform at New Cross Gate station, seen from the road overbridge, looked rather different in this view of 13 May 1980. All the sidings and their contents have long gone, the bay platform is now a through road, electrification is third and not fourth rail, and the fleet of A60 stock trains, then still in unpainted aluminium livery, are being withdrawn from service altogether. The station fabric survives.* John Glover

Left: *At Forest Hill on 12 April 2010 a footbridge plus lifts is being constructed to provide access from the ticket office (up side, left) to the down side. The only access available previously between the two was a subway under the track, for which numerous steps need to be negotiated.* John Glover

CHAPTER 15: **NORTH LONDON INFRASTRUCTURE**

Right: Stratford Low Level on 12 September 2009, showing works under way on the conversion of part of the North Woolwich branch to reflect Docklands Light Railway standards. This part of the station is now shared only with the Jubilee Line of London Underground, with no National Rail presence. John Glover

Below: This 10 February 2010 picture shows the work going on to extend the westbound platform at Willesden Junction High Level over the Low Level lines to enable it to take four-car trains. A direct pedestrian route to the Low Level station footbridge is in the process of being constructed. John Glover

The infrastructure works on the North London line were required for a number of reasons, which in the end amounted to a very substantial programme for Network Rail.

The first need was to accommodate services from the East London Line on the formation as far as Highbury & Islington, which was a completely new demand and required four-tracking of the section west of Dalston Junction. There are no running connections between the two paired sets of lines, one being AC and the other DC electrified.

These had to be reconciled with the requirements of through freight traffic, not only in respect of that moving at present, but also the increased traffic due to the expansion of Felixstowe and Harwich. Still in the future are works at what was Thameshaven on the Tilbury line, to turn that into a major port. Much of what was originally a four-track line between Dalston and Camden Road was reduced to the southern pair used by the electrified passenger services (the North London No 2 lines), and the remaining pair (North London No 1 lines) on the north side were converted to a long single-track section electrified at 25kV AC. Recent works required an element of reinstatement of four-tracking, though in the final plan this was not carried out over the whole section. It might be noted that there was no regular passenger train usage of the No 1 lines, and most of the former platforms were demolished.

Network Rail, North London

An early part of the North London Line work was gauge enhancement to freight W10 loading gauge to take 9ft 6in containers on standard flat wagons. This included the stretch through the notorious Hampstead Heath Tunnel. Unfortunately, when the tunnel was blockaded in the early 1990s to facilitate the movement of Regional Eurostars (which in the end was abortive), clearance for large containers did not feature. Thus

there was an 11-week closure in 2008 for this work to be done by Nuttall and slab track was installed.

Network Rail appointed Carillion as the main contractor for the works east of Gospel Oak towards Stratford. The work included four-tracking between Boleyn Road (Dalston) and the approach to Camden Road. Here a mix of two, three or four tracks was to be replaced.

Retaining walls were to be stabilised and a leaking sewer under the tracks replaced. Track lowering under bridges was undertaken, to allow for overhead electrification, and provision made for the introduction of the service from Dalston Junction towards Highbury & Islington.

Further work was the upgrading of the power supply and the removal of the remaining third rail on these parts of the North London lines. Thus the only place where third rail can now be found is on the Acton Central to Richmond section and south of the M4 bridge on the West London Line. Thirty station platforms were extended to accommodate four-car trains where necessary.

Resignalling by Atkins was to take place concurrently. Control of the Willesden Junction-Stratford and Gospel Oak-Barking sections was to be transferred to the Upminster Integrated Electronic Control Centre (IECC) and telecommunications upgraded.

Core section

On the core section of the route, the railway is in a constricted cutting with brick retaining walls and difficult road access. Carillion used works trains, loaded off-site, to bring in the plant required, and also for spoil removal and the provision of fresh ballast.

Other works have been the completely new platforms at Caledonian Road & Barnsbury, Canonbury and Highbury & Islington, together with associated footbridges and lifts, secondary means of escape at some stations for fire regulations purposes, and a new Channelsea loop on the western exit from Stratford to allow freight trains to clear the Great Eastern main line even if they cannot be accepted immediately onto the North London Line.

A new turnback siding for West London trains was provided at Willesden Junction High Level, avoiding the time taken in running to Kensal Rise and back for a similar facility. This is part of the works needed to operate 4tph to Clapham Junction.

Also required is the doubling of the Latchmere curve at Clapham Junction. This is severely speed-restricted and an impediment to the quick entry and exit of trains from Willesden Junction to the single platform. They of course also need to reverse direction before returning.

TfL's programme of station improvements, such as upgraded CCTV, public address, lighting and passenger information screens, new signs, general refurbishment, and new lifts at some locations has continued in tandem with the line upgrades.

T&H

Underbridge and track upgrading, and structure gauge widening, has made the Gospel Oak-Barking line suitable for higher W10 gauge containers. £18.5 million from the government's Transport Innovation Fund was being complemented by £16.5 million from Network Rail. Thus this line has become an alternative route to the North London for freight traffic between Stratford and Willesden. This ability was used extensively during the enforced closure to all traffic of the Gospel Oak to

Above: The bridge leading to the station platforms at Kilburn High Road is still covered and some attempt has been made to present a clean and tidy appearance. What standards do passengers expect from a suburban station of this nature? On 12 September 2009 the approaching train is formed of No 313121. John Glover

Above: *Stratford Low Level on 12 September 2009, showing works under way on the conversion of part of the North Woolwich branch to reflect Docklands Light Railway standards. This part of the station is now shared only with the Jubilee Line of London Underground, with no National Rail presence.* John Glover

Stratford section in 2010 for extensive track and signalling work.

The signalling system here has also been renewed and the block sections broken up. This allows TfL to double the passenger service frequencies from 2tph to 4tph, although the implementation was delayed due to the late delivery of the new Class 172 trains. The Mayor would like to see Gospel Oak-Barking electrified.

Disruption

Inevitably, carrying out work of this nature and extent meant a whole succession of line closures, some of them lasting a matter of months. There was no rail service at all between Gospel Oak and Stratford from 20 February to 31 May 2010, a period of 14 weeks; as the explanatory leaflet announced cheerfully, 'It is possible that further full week closures may be required later this year.' In any event, weekend rail services had become a rarity. TfL provided replacement bus services as appropriate.

The planned London Overground service disruptions starting in 2009 were as follows:

* No full service on the Gospel Oak to Barking line at weekends from 7 February until 26 October 2009
* Full line closure for 11 full weekends and five Sundays
* Closure between South Tottenham and Barking for 20 Saturdays

* No service on the line from Richmond to Stratford on Sundays from 19 April to 21 December 2009
* No service between Gospel Oak and Stratford from 25 December 2009 until 4 January 2010
* No service between Queen's Park and Wembley Central every day between 25 December 2009 and 1 January 2010.

The cynic might comment that if the railway can be closed with impunity for the sorts of periods that have been commonplace on this group of services, is it really necessary to provide it at all? Readers are perhaps unlikely to agree with such a view, but is it so unreasonable in the hard-nosed world in which we live? That is a challenge that the railway industry needs to face.

There is, however, a pot of gold at the end of it all. 'When we have completed the upgrade ... we will be able to run trains at least every 20 minutes on the entire network and in many places this will be improved, with some sections getting trains every 7-8 minutes.' (TfL, December 2009)

Stratford

At Stratford, Network Rail undertook upgrade works at the station and the tracks that serve the London 2012 Olympic Games and Paralympic Games and new developments in the area. The benefits of the completed works include:

* nine new lifts that make the station fully accessible for all passengers
* two new station entrances that greatly improve passenger flow
* new stairs that improve access and reduce congestion
* improved transport links and new subways that make interchanges easier
* Stratford station and the Stratford City Development are now fully integrated via a new footbridge.

These works were funded by the Olympic Delivery Authority.

North London upgrade

Considerable care was taken by Network Rail to keep neighbourhoods informed of the work going on to upgrade the Overground network. Thus for the three-month line closure east of Gospel Oak in the first part of 2010, a letter to residents explained that the closure would allow Network Rail to carry out major track and signalling work as well as platform lengthening, access improvement and some refurbishment work.

First, there was the general work along the route, which consisted of the installation of structures and equipment associated with electrification. This included concrete foundations, steel structures and wiring. Then, similarly, that associated with signalling, which included the gantries and the signals themselves. A second phase with signalling was to test and commission it at the end of the line closure. This was described to local residents as a quieter occupation, perhaps indicating that some of the other work might be a little noisy.

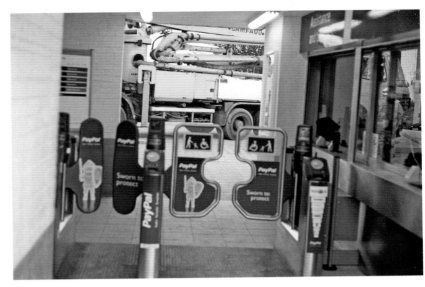

The work would involve general construction activity including delivery of materials, excavation, removal of spoil, pouring of concrete, the use of cranes and other machinery, and alterations to track and signalling. A number of track access points, some new, were established to allow work to proceed. The use of road-rail excavators gave the opportunity for relatively remote access, which could only be used effectively on a railway where engineering interests had complete possession. Railways in highly urbanised areas can have considerable problems.

Work compounds

There were also work compounds where equipment and materials could be stored. Thus, at the site known as Gifford Street embankment, according to Network

Above: *The new order on the North London Line is a staffed ticket office (right) and ticket barriers at some locations. This is Canonbury on 10 February 2010. The large contractors' vehicle outside is a reflection of the scale of track work that was then under way here.* John Glover

Left: *The widening of Boleyn Bridge west of Dalston Kingsland station was a major operation, as can be seen from this view of 4 June 2010. The road was completely closed for some time while the bridge was widened.* John Glover

Rail, 'The availability of suitable land space in this area of London is limited, meaning that there are no other alternatives.' Well, that's clear enough! This area is on the eastern side of the East Coast Main Line, where HS1 emerges from its tunnel from Dagenham and the North London passes overhead. The site had been used previously by contractors for railway works. This perhaps emphasises the importance for the railway of trying to keep the local community on its side.

Considerable care was taken about the effects of the modernisation works on the residents all along the North London Line. Thus: 'We intend to work from 8am until 10pm, seven days a week. An additional half-hour will be used before and after each shift for preparation and demobilisation. There will also be occasional work outside these hours for limited periods during the closure; however, this will be kept to a minimum and machinery will not be used. This work will only involve a small number of site personnel and the use of hand-held tools to complete testing and commissioning.

'Work will be carried out under section 61 of the Control of Pollution Act, 1974. All staff on site will be briefed and supervised to reduce noise and keep disruption to a minimum.'

Activities

The key activities, from east to west, were as follows:

Dalston Kingsland: Both platforms needed to be lengthened at the western end, for which the reconstruction of the Boleyn Road bridge was required. This involved the removal of the main section of the bridge and the supporting abutments, and rebuilding the bridge to the west of the previous position. All services (cabling, drainage, etc) then needed to be diverted to the new bridge. Boleyn Road bridge was then reopened to local traffic.

Such work involved delivery of materials, excavation, removing of spoil, pouring of concrete, use of cranes and other machinery, and adjustments to track and signalling. Heavier work was needed for removal of the previous bridge. There was a work compound and the bridge was closed for all purposes to access the site. It might be added that the platform extensions required were 19 metres.

Canonbury: A new platform needed to be built on the north side of the station, with the existing island platform widened (the north side of this was previously disused). The existing footbridge and staircases were altered to suit, and a new footbridge and stairs to the new north-side platform were constructed at the western end of the station. Lifts and an emergency fire exit were installed. This is the main location for interchange between the North and East London lines; it is the obvious choice for those travelling from east to south, or vice versa, and is simpler than Highbury & Islington for other users as all trains to the East London leave from the same platform.

Between Canonbury and Highbury & Islington: A new railway-only communications mast was installed. This is part of a new system to allow secure, direct and continuous communication between the train driver and the signaller. Thus in the event of an incident in the area all trains can be advised to stop immediately, to guard against any further incidents occurring. Minor incidents can be resolved more quickly, and more accurate and up-to-date information will be available to staff and customers alike. The local problem was to find a location that would give 100% coverage of this section of the North London Line. Canonbury station is in a deep cutting, with mature trees on each side of the track, and the 15-metre-high mast was felt to be a reasonable addition to station lighting standards and overhead electrification.

Also in this area was the land prepared for the East London Line connection from Dalston Junction. This required new pointwork in association with the track separation; joint running is not intended, and the track layout and the electrification systems prevent it anyway. The DC lines have been extended on the south side of the four-track formation to terminate in the two platforms, again on the south side of the formation at Highbury & Islington.

Highbury & Islington: Major works were needed here to re-create a four-platform station from two and a bit (the 'bit' was Platform 7 on the westbound freight lines, for occasional use by short trains only, which had to be AC electrics or diesel-powered). The platforms on the south side used formerly by the passenger services are now dedicated terminal platforms for the East London Line operation and hence third rail only; the others are in effect new construction, with AC overhead electrification. Access improvements saw an extension to the station concourse and alterations to the staircases and the installation of a lift. A new interchange bridge was built at the western end of the platforms, with an emergency exit. Track, signalling and electrification works generally took place in the station area and on either side.

Between Highbury & Islington and Caledonian Road & Barnsbury: Sewer and drainage systems replacement were needed, together with track replacement on the new formation. Isolation transformers were installed near the Liverpool Road overbridge to protect the interface between the upgraded London Overground DC lines and others at AC. This work involved the excavation and removal of soil using digging machinery and wagons, delivery of materials and equipment to site, construction of concrete foundations and permanent fencing, and installation and connection of the electrical equipment.

Caledonian Road & Barnsbury: Of the two side platforms for the tracks on the south side, that for westbound trains was taken out of use except for access to the new island platform. This uses the former eastbound platform, plus new construction to make it

an island. Trains thus call at a single island platform which is used in both directions. A new footbridge has been installed, together with lifts.

Between Caledonian Road & Barnsbury and Camden Road: The rail underbridge crossing Camley Road needed replacement. Temporary supports were constructed for the existing bridge, which was then dismantled, half at a time, to allow the main construction work to take place. The construction included utility cable work, pouring of concrete structures and placement of pre-cast concrete beams. Some of this required the use of a crane. The newly constructed deck was place temporarily at a higher level while further work was undertaken. It was then slid into place, followed by finishing and refurbishment activities.

A work compound was established underneath the bridge on the main roadway, and was used in conjunction with the existing compound adjacent. This required a road diversion to be put in place. The compound was used to access the worksite, the signing on and off of staff, delivery and storage of construction materials, a holding area for plant, and the use of a crane for the construction stage.

Camden Road: Platform extensions were required, although the previous ones had not been demolished as was commonplace elsewhere.

Kentish Town West: Platform extensions were the main work here, at the west end of both. Here the work involved delivery of materials to the site, provision of concrete foundations, construction of a structural steel frame, refurbishment of the brick arches beneath, and the erection of fences and barriers. In this case, steelwork was to be delivered by road and lifted by road crane up to track level. This station, like many others on the North London Line, is built on viaduct.

Gospel Oak: The westbound North London Line platform only needed to be extended here. Considerable information was provided on the access arrangements for plant and equipment, staff transport arrangements, and how road/rail excavators would find their way onto the track.

*Above: This is the western end of the extended Dalston Kingsland platforms required for four-car trains, looking under the now widened Boleyn Road bridge on 4 June 2010. No 378022 in three-car form is approaching over the newly realigned tracks with a train bound for Stratford. Dalston Western Junction signalbox is now visible from the platforms, though it closed on 18 December 2010 when control passed to Upminster/ECC.
John Glover*

NORTH LONDON INFRASTRUCTURE

Right: *The work site at Dalston Junction, seen from a passing train on 12 December 2009. Note the road access, which is to be retained for long-term use. The location is in the vee between the North London Line and Dalston Junction station.* John Glover

Hampstead Heath: Here, as elsewhere, ticket sales points had to be provided from new or renovated to ensure that suitable accommodation was available for staff.

Finchley Road & Frognal: Both platforms were extended to allow four-car operation. This required clearance of vegetation, moving cables, providing concrete foundations, constructing platform walls and infilling with gravel. An emergency escape route was provided from the extended platforms; at the other end of the station there are steps up to the road and nothing else apart from the mouth of Hampstead Heath tunnel.

West Hampstead: This station is in a cutting, and both platforms needed to be extended at the west end. For the north-side (eastbound) platform, this required the prior construction of a piled wall to support the embankment, replacing the former stone-in-wire-basket supports.

Brondesbury: This was another western-end platform extension job. Notably, it was pointed out that as the railway on this section would be closed for 24 hours most Sundays, this would be Network Rail's busiest day. That required Sunday to be used to carry out any work immediately adjacent to the tracks and also resulted in Sunday deliveries of materials.

Brondesbury Park: Here, as in many other places, platform extension work (at the western end) was supplemented with the installation of new signalling and equipment cabinets.

Kensal Rise: Both platforms were extended at the Willesden Junction end and the stairs on the eastbound

platform replaced with a wider set to reduce congestion with two-way flows. A new emergency exit was also provided.

East of Willesden Junction: A new turnback siding was constructed between the two tracks of the North London Line, located between the Harrow Road bridge and Kensal Rise Junction. The work entailed remodelling the overhead power lines, light sheet piling by road-rail machines, replacing the track drainage, and installing two turnouts to allow trains to enter and exit the siding. Materials were delivered via the Station Road entrance.

Willesden Junction: Complex station rebuilding affected both the High Level and Low Level parts of the station. The work was aimed at permitting the accommodation of four-car trains at the two High Level platforms and the central reversing bay at Low Level. Additionally, a new interchange pathway would be constructed from the extended platforms at the Stratford end of the station, by subway to the steps at the end of the existing bridge leading down to Platforms 1 and 2 of the Low Level.

At High Level, the problems of platform extension were acute, due to the existing platforms at the Richmond end of the station ending at the bridge where the West Coast Main Line passes underneath the North London, and at the other by bridge reconstruction in the past that truncated the previously adequate-length platforms where the North London passed over the tracks as they entered Low Level. Thus widening of the steel bridge was called for to allow a 25-metre platform extension on both lines, and the other works detailed.

To allow the Low Level Platform 2 bay to be extended, other platform buildings beyond the end of

the bay as it existed previously were demolished and rebuilt on the filled-in site where the second long disused bay platform once was.

This general construction work required the delivery and removal of materials and excavation and the removal of spoil, together with adjustments to track and signalling. The whole of the signalling between Acton and Stratford was renewed, to provide increased line capacity.

Acton Central: Works here were confined to extension of both platforms at the Richmond end of the station, as there is a level crossing at the Willesden Junction end. This is one of only two on the whole of what has become the London Overground network, the other being a short distance away at Bollo Lane, beyond South Acton. Platform work involved the usual shrub clearance and the moving of signalling cables, the installation of steel piles to support the platforms, the erecting of walls and the placing of concrete planks for the platform surfaces.

South Acton: Platform extensions here were made at the eastern end. To assist access, a new road/rail access point was installed at the nearby Bollo Lane Crossing (on the line to Gunnersbury). The line in the

vicinity of Acton Central/South Acton is more or less at grade, which makes access for staff, plant and materials much easier than where it is in deep cutting or on bridges.

When the Network Rail work set out above was completed, Transport for London refurbished many of the station premises to bring them up to standard.

West London and West London Extension

A new station was opened at Shepherds Bush on the West London Line on 28 September 2008. This was linked with the major reconstruction of Shepherds Bush Central Line station – the two entrances now face each other – and the huge Westfield shopping development, which also saw Wood Lane station opened on the Hammersmith & City Line on 12 October 2008.

This was followed by Imperial Wharf, opened on 29 September 2009, a £7.8 million project funded by St George plc (£4.8 million), London boroughs (£2 million) and TfL (£1 million). The station is linked to residential, office and leisure development in the area. It is on the site of Sands End gasworks and was originally to be known as Chelsea Harbour.

Above: *No 313108 arrives at Willesden Junction High Level with a service for Clapham Junction to find a remarkably full platform on 12 September 2009. Why the interest? Almost certainly, these good people are on their way to the Westfield shopping centre, for which they will alight at Shepherds Bush. Another Westfield has been created outside Stratford station. One might note that traffic of this nature is likely to be more enduring and hence more valuable than that for a once-in-a-lifetime sporting event.* John Glover

CHAPTER 16: **ORBITING LONDON**

Attention then centred on the restoration of a long-discarded link towards the South Central. It was found possible to create a direct route to the 'other' South Central line from London Bridge, which could take East London Line trains to Peckham Rye.

Wimbledon or Clapham Junction?

Then what? Possibilities included joining the South London route towards Denmark Hill, Clapham High Street, Wandsworth Road, Battersea Park and Victoria, or turning south towards Tulse Hill. This then offered further alternatives, and Wimbledon was one of the possible destinations that was then preferred. However, it would still not result in an orbital service, since a trip by District Line Underground to West Brompton would then be needed to reach the West London Line south from Willesden Junction. Alternatively, National Rail could be used to reach Clapham Junction.

It will be appreciated that while the various alternatives might appear reasonably straightforward, train paths have to be found and conflicting movements dealt with sufficiently robustly so that a workable and reliable timetable can be devised. It also has to fit with the franchising commitments of other operators on the routes concerned, mostly Southern Railway but also First Capital Connect's Thameslink services. If the intention is to run an all-day 4tph service, this is a far from minor undertaking.

Consideration of the South London Line in more depth also showed how the complex junctions south of Clapham Junction could be used constructively. If, on leaving Wandsworth Road, the service could be diverted to the west via what are known as the Ludgate Lines, the service could reach the north side of the Clapham Junction complex, and in particular Platform 2 now used by the Overground service from Willesden Junction. That could complete the orbital route.

Construction works

The East London scheme made substantial changes to the West Croydon and Crystal Palace services, so that most of them became an appendage to the East London Line. The service provided runs south from Surrey Quays to the site of a long-abandoned junction, where a new 40mph link is forged to the South London Line proper. Specifically, the new 1.3km link is from a re-created Silwood Junction on the East London (where a new flyover has been provided for the northbound East London Line from New Cross Gate as part of the Phase 1 works) to the former Old Kent Road Junction on the Brighton line, north of Queens Road Peckham. Creating this link would be the main engineering works to be undertaken, with work on site starting in the summer of 2011. These works are TfL-led, with TfL owning this part of the new infrastructure.

The earlier work at Silwood Junction meant that building the link later would have minimal effects on the services already operating. One of the complications is that some of the disused trackbed is presently used as a cycleway, for which alternative routeing would be necessary. The principal construction is the new bridge across Surrey Canal Road. The railway has to provide a 5.3-metre clearance for road vehicles beneath the bridge deck, while at the same time passing beneath the Network Rail viaducts 280 metres distant. That results in a track gradient of 1 in 29 for the railway, and demonstrates how building for the exclusive use of services of this nature can use very different parameters than would be necessary for either high-speed operation or freight. (It may be noted here that the Primrose Hill dive-under of the early 1920s utilised a 1 in 35 gradient, which might have to be negotiated from a standing start.)

Old Kent Road Junction

Trains then progress from Old Kent Road Junction via the existing stations at Queens Road Peckham, Peckham Rye, Denmark Hill, Clapham High Street and Wandsworth Road, to Factory Junction, just beyond Wandsworth Road station. Here, rather than take the 'Atlantic Line' as at present to Battersea Park, they instead follow and keep to the down 'Ludgate Line'. This passes beneath all the main lines to the east of Clapham Junction station – as many as 12 parallel tracks plus a siding or two for the carriage washing plant. From this the trains emerge on the north side of the entire formation, beyond the South Western Windsor lines, which positions them ideally to enter Platform 2, where they terminate.

Below: The construction of the link from Silwood Junction to Old Kent Road Junction was well under way on 8 September 2011, with the new formation seen here approaching the Southern line between South Bermondsey and Queen's Road, Peckham stations. John Glover

Clapham Junction

Early ideas intended to use both sides of what was originally an island platform here but which later had the tracks to Platform 1 removed. These plans were discarded due to the asset condition of the one-time 'banana arches' below. However, Platform 2 is long enough to take ten-car trains, and is separated from the tracks for Platform 3 (up Windsor Slow) by a middle road. Consequently, the decision was made to create a second platform by in effect dividing the present one lengthways. Thus trains at the east end of Platform 2 are those for the West London Line, Willesden Junction and beyond, and those at the west end, reached from the middle road, are for New Cross Gate and Dalston Junction.

Each service thus has a separate single platform and there will be no through running, although the trains in each platform will later be very close to each other again in the Dalston area. Quite apart from the practical reasons why an 'outer circle' type operation is undesirable, there is the little matter of electrification standards. Thus the services to Dalston via Willesden use the Class 378/2 units with dual-voltage capability, while the Class 378/1 units for services to Dalston via New Cross Gate are fitted for third rail DC only. To be fair to TfL, the Class 378/1s do have the capability of being converted in future to dual-voltage specification should this be required.

Battersea Park and London Bridge

One loss is the direct link between Battersea Park and Wandsworth Road, for which no replacement rail link is to be provided other than via Clapham Junction. While this is perhaps unfortunate, the main platforms at Battersea Park are to be extended to accommodate ten-car trains as part of the capacity expansion programme on the Southern. This work will mean extending them to the north (towards Victoria), and as

a result the junction that gives access to the South London will itself be blocked.

Surrey Canal Road

An additional station was proposed for Surrey Canal Road, close to the Millwall Football Club ground. As the site is on an embankment, the substantial capital costs would be in the order of £10 million. How substantial and extensive would the works need to be? The Millwall ground has a capacity of 20,000, so the premises could on occasion be swamped. It has not proved possible to secure all the funding needed for a station here, so passive provision only will be made with the help of the London Borough of Lewisham. Later construction on an operational railway would result in costs rising further.

South Bermondsey station, not part of London Overground, is on the west side of the football ground, while Surrey Canal Road station would, if built, be on the south side. Both would have similar catchment areas.

Brixton station

The South London Line crosses the A23, Brixton Road, within sight of the Underground station, which on the face of it suggests that an additional station serving this area would be a good idea. However, as so often in railway matters, it is not that simple. The nearby Atlantic Road viaduct is extremely high, as it takes the South London Line over the top of the South Eastern lines and Brixton (National Rail) station, which itself is on a viaduct above the street and the entrance to London Underground's Brixton station. Furthermore, the South London Line on both sides of the viaduct has curves and gradients to match.

Thus, good idea it might be, but costs, affordability and practical issues rule it out as a serious proposition. If the Surrey Canal Road station seemed expensive at £10 million, the bill for a station here is estimated at roundly £40 million.

Above: *Trains cross at Haggerston; here we see a northbound No 378142 (right) and a southbound No 378145 (left) on 28 April 2010. The stations at platform level have only the necessary attributes of shelter, lighting and some protection from the wind.* John Glover

User considerations

It is not possible to make changes of such a nature without causing some problems to existing users. Thus a diversion of South London Line services to Clapham Junction would result in the withdrawal of services between Wandsworth Road and Battersea Park, so the direct link to Victoria would be lost. Those at Peckham Rye and Denmark Hill would still have their Southeastern services to Victoria, while Southern Railway offers other services towards London Bridge from Peckham Rye, Queens Road Peckham and South Bermondsey.

It can also be argued that one of the aims of the diverted service is to improve connectional opportunities, and so in many ways it does. Clapham Junction in particular offers a huge range of destinations that are directly served, while interchanging to the Jubilee Line at Canada Water or the Hammersmith & City and District at Whitechapel gives at least as many opportunities as previously.

The main problem is perhaps that of change, and the disinclination of some people, maybe many, to accept that it must happen if there is to be progress. Even the statutory user groups such as London Travelwatch have this problem, in a rather different sense. Their job is to look after the interests of passengers, but while this clearly includes the existing

Above: The ticket machines at Haggerston station. The need for a ticket office as such when so many users have Oyster is becoming less certain, and London Overground is moving towards all-purpose members of staff with multiple skills rather than just issuing tickets on demand. John Glover

Right: The Elliptical Switchback, a mural at Haggerston station, is seen by passengers as they make their way from the ticket office area to the stairs leading to the platforms. This printed tile mural was commissioned by Rail for London. John Glover

Right: The passenger needs to know details of the next train and this admirably clear signage at Willesden Junction sets it out for Platform 3. But although the next train may be on time, when exactly is it due? Never mind, this is the Underground, and the following Overground train will be along in just over seven minutes at 11:51. John Glover

Above: There is much spare space at Crystal Palace, and additional platforms and turnback roads have been introduced for the London Overground services. This is the scene before the new services started on 12 April 2010. John Glover

Left: The original entrances to Crystal Palace station seen in 2005, when it was hoped that they and the ticket hall behind them would be restored for public use. This is a fine station, but as it is really two separate stations side by side there are a few shortcomings.
John Glover

passengers, what about the nebulous ones of the future who will use the new facilities that are not available at the present time?

How then can the longer-term benefits for what seems likely to be considerably greater numbers of people, who in effect don't exist at the moment, be given due consideration? Short-term matters are important, but they do need to be balanced against future plans and expectations, and the benefits that they are designed to bring.

The extension from Surrey Quays to Clapham Junction opens in late 2012.

Above: *This is the new railway bridge over Shoreditch High Street, from which the Overground station takes its name, looking north on 28 April 2010. Yes, double-deck buses will go under it, despite the single-deck articulated version looking quite tight!* John Glover

Right: *This is the bridge carrying the line from New Cross Gate over the Southern tracks and through the London Overground depot area, as seen on 28 June 2010. Grade separation using devices such as this is essential when high service frequencies are desired.* John Glover

CHAPTER 17: **NEW TRAINS AND SERVICES**

For all London Overground services, new rolling stock is entering service, and this is now described. A comparison is also made of the major features of the electric stock with two of its predecessors.

Class 378

The Class 378 electric units are a variety of the 'Electrostar' units from Bombardier at Derby, as used by both Southern Railway and Southeastern, and also c2c. Named 'Capitalstar' by TfL, these are 20-metre vehicles, each 2.8 metres wide and with a maximum speed of 75mph.

The original £223 million contract between Bombardier and Transport for London provided for 24 AC/DC three-car units for the North London lines (including Euston-Watford and the West London Line) and 20 DC third-rail only four-car units for the East London Line (including the Southern extensions). This amounted to a total of 152 cars. There was also an option to purchase up to 216 cars in total.

A subsequent order for 36 additional vehicles costing £36 million extended the three-car North London sets to four cars and provided an additional three four-car trains for the East London Line. Those delivered as Class 378/0 three-car AC/DC units are

renumbered Class 378/2 when the extra vehicle taking them to four cars is added. Both contracts include fleet maintenance by the builders, and this is undertaken at the newly constructed depot at New Cross Gate.

Two further orders increased the number of Class 378/2 dual-voltage units by seven (28 vehicles), thus exhausting the earlier option, then again for another three units (12 vehicles).

Thus, with all the orders complete, the TfL fleet of Class 378 trains is as shown in Table 17.1.

These trains were to be purchased outright by TfL, but in 2008 ideas changed and they are leased from a newly formed rolling stock company (ROSCO), QW Rail Leasing Ltd. This is a joint venture between National Australia Bank and Sumitomo Mitsui Banking Corporation. 'This will avoid capital expenditure and release millions of pounds for reinvestment,' said an enthusiastic TfL press release – but wasn't that always

Above: *No 313117 is seen on 12 September 2009 at the new Stratford platforms for North London services. The bridge across the whole of the railway is for visitors to the London Olympics in 2012 arriving at Stratford International and is designed to keep such crowds well clear of domestic operations.* John Glover

Table 17.1: Class 378 orders, June 2010			
Class	**378/1** **DC only**	**378/2** **AC/DC**	**Total**
No of vehicles	80	148	228
No of units	20	37	57

Above: *The new Class 378 'Capitalstar' units were becoming noticeable by the autumn of 2009; this is No 378016 leaving Willesden Junction High Level for Stratford on 12 September 2009. Originally three-car units as seen here, additional vehicles to make the original series sets up to four cars were ordered later.* John Glover

Right: *The Class 378s are fitted with Dellner couplers, seen here on the front of No 378142. A multiplicity of coupling types can make for difficulties if one train fails and the succeeding one is unable to 'push it out'. The answer of course is to make trains so reliable that they never do fail, though compatible coupling arrangements wouldn't be a bad idea either.* John Glover

one of the benefits of leasing as opposed to ownership? The leasing company bears the risk of disposing of the depreciated fleet after the lease is terminated. TfL bears the risk of the fleet performance and maintenance during the term of the lease, but heavy maintenance remains with the manufacturer, Bombardier.

The financial consequences for a number of TfL's risks are passed on to third parties. Thus the penalty for late train delivery was borne by Bombardier, and London Overground operator LOROL can be penalised if non-structural conditions in the vehicles fall below the standards agreed with TfL.

The lease gives TfL use of the trains until 2027, or longer if it wishes. This differs from the normal rolling stock lease for Train Operating Companies on the national network, which lasts only as long as their franchises. The terms of the lease will not have to be renegotiated by TfL when the contract expires.

Principal features

While the general construction of the Class 378 series might be similar to the other 'Electrostar' builds, these trains include some significant differences. The principal features are as follows:

* Three or four cars per set as originally built, though all later became four cars when platform-lengthening works had been completed
* Standard layout of Driving Motor Open, Motor Second Open, (Pantograph) Trailer Second Open, and Driving Motor Open
* Two pairs of double sliding doors on each body side, rather than plug doors, for speed and reliability of operation
* Radio systems fitted are National Radio Network (for North London Line and thus not DC-only units), Cab Secure Radio (for Euston-Watford, West London and South London lines) and GSM-R (for East London Line TfL network)
* Electricity regeneration to grid when braking, saving on energy consumption
* Internal and external CCTV monitoring by the driver
* London Underground-type tripcocks
* Very wide walk-through facility between all three/ four cars, but no end gangways
* Option for passenger control of doors released/ secured by driver (preferred), or all on one side opened/closed simultaneously by driver
* Tube-style longitudinal and fairly hard seating only, with the priority seats for the disabled distinguished by colour

Left: *No 378021 arrives at Kensal Rise on 15 April 2010 with a train for Richmond. Some considerable work on the station premises is under way here as can be seen, and a side entrance to the station has been created (right).* John Glover

Table 17.2: Electric multiple-unit types compared

TOPS class	501	313/1	378/0
Introduced	1957	1976	2008
No of cars	3	3	3
Length of train	52.46m	59.52m	61.06m
No of seats	256	232	112
Electrification	DC only	DC/AC	DC/AC
No of units	57	27	24

Notes:

* The Class 501 centre trailers were later rebuilt to open saloon specification, which reduced the seating to 240 (or 242). They were frequently used in pairs to make six cars.
* The Class 313/1s had extra shoegear added for their North London use, and seating was reduced to 202. The fleet total includes the three Class 508 DC-only units transferred from Merseyside.
* The Class 378/0s were built originally as shown, but later reclassified Class 378/2 with an extra vehicle. The seating includes six tip-up seats. The three-car versions have been shown, to provide a direct comparison.

* Very large standing capacity
* Full air-conditioning
* Real-time passenger information
* No luggage racks
* Option of adding more cars within each unit should circumstances warrant, but this depends crucially on the ability of platform lengths, widths and access arrangements to cope

* External liveries are a variation of that used on London Underground, with orange passenger doors and the obligatory yellow ends replacing red in both cases. Internally, a neutral beige appearance looks distinctly municipal, but that is perhaps only to be expected.

The first dual-voltage Class 378/0s entered service on the North London Line on 29 July 2009, and test running on the East London Line with a Class 378/1 (DC only) began on 5 October 2009 when a train departed from New Cross Gate depot and travelled to Dalston Junction. Passenger operation of the Class 378/1s began on 27 April 2010 for a period of what was termed preview running.

The new stock is capable of working as units of three, four, five or six cars, so longer trains formed of one lengthened unit are a possibility.

Stock comparisons

As has been indicated, ideas of what makes the ideal rolling stock design have varied as the years progressed. Table 17.2 shows the basic statistics of the three main classes of electric multiple-unit that have been used over the years on this group of services. They are shown in as-built condition, but see also notes below.

The most remarkable feature is how the number of seats has diminished, to the extent that the Class 378s have only 44% of the seats provided in their 1957 counterparts, in a set of vehicles that is 16% longer. To some extent this is a reflection on changing social preferences, and days when the provision of a seat was of the highest priority. Whether or not the reductions seen here can be classified as desirable depends in part

on average journey length. Those travelling a couple of
stops only will have a different outlook from those
travelling in from West Croydon to perhaps Shoreditch
High Street.

Fewer seats means more space for standing
passengers, and those seemingly vast child
pushchairs. The North London Line, especially at the
Stratford end, is very busy, so more standing space is
to be welcomed. What level of new traffic will the
other lines attract over time? It is noticeable that
significant numbers of passengers do not bother to
sit down at all, but that in turn can make it quite
difficult for alighting passengers to fight their way to
the doors.

This is a Metro-type service, with frequencies that
are around 4tph. Trains at about 15-minute intervals
are not really frequent enough for people to turn up
without first consulting a timetable, but it is certainly a
step in that direction.

The reaction of the travelling public will be awaited
with interest.

Class 172

The Gospel Oak-Barking service is also provided with
a 4tph service, but with diesel trains. A new build of
eight air-conditioned two-car trains of Class 172/0
'Turbostar' diesel stock was delivered from 2010.
These 16 vehicles have similarities with other orders
related to Chiltern Railways and London Midland,
which will take the total construction programme up
to 93 vehicles in two- or three-car sets.

Maximum speed is again 75mph but in longer
23-metre vehicles than the Class 378. They replace the
Class 150 units used in recent years, which were built
in the late 1980s and were beginning to show their
age. As for their features, a comment found on the
internet made the following observation about the
Class 172s: 'Transverse 2+2 seating, wide high-back
thick-cushioned seats, luggage racks, able to see out of
the windows during the journey. My, how very civilised.

'How I wish Rail for London had chosen this
interior layout for the rest of the LO operations,

rather than the oppressive and uncomfortable Class 378s.'

As discussed, the interiors are not everybody's idea of an ideal train, but making space to squeeze on as many people as possible is one way of attacking the service capacity problem.

The Class 172/0s are financed conventionally through the Angel Trains ROSCO, leased by the operator, London Overground Rail Operations Ltd. It is no secret, however, that London Overground would wish to see this line electrified. That would give new opportunities for service provision, particularly but not exclusively west of Gospel Oak.

East London opening

The East London Line service was opened by the Mayor of London, Boris Johnson, between Dalston Junction and New Cross/New Cross Gate (only) on 27 April 2010, the first train leaving Dalston Junction at 12:05. This operation was termed a preview service, operating between 07:00 and 20:00 on Mondays to Fridays only, with services running at 4tph (two each from Dalston Junction to New Cross and New Cross Gate). Weekend working was introduced on 15/16 May.

The service from Dalston Junction to New Cross, West Croydon and Crystal Palace commenced on Sunday, 23 May 2010, with the start of the new National Railways timetable. The full Metro-style service commenced on the Monday, running from 05:40 until approximately 00:15. The full timetable showed the frequency of trains over the section south of Dalston Junction increase to 12tph, or every five minutes, proceeding successively to New Cross, West Croydon, New Cross Gate and Crystal Palace.

Thus Phase 1 of the scheme was now complete, with the Phase 1a extension to Highbury & Islington following on 28 February 2011.

Orbital route

The Overground service forms an orbital route right around London. Phase 2, which was not authorised until February 2009, completed the orbital network from Surrey Quays to Clapham Junction in 2012. Service levels over the core section rise to 16tph with the completion of Phase 2.

The completed scheme allows, either directly or with a single change of trains, journeys such as Clapham Junction to Dalston and Crystal Palace to West Hampstead. It is thought that rapid demand growth on parts of the Overground in future years could justify investment in longer five-car or even six-car trains.

Thus, in addition to the services mentioned earlier, the services provided by the East (and South) London lines are as follows:

* Dalston Junction to New Cross/West Croydon/ Crystal Palace (21 stations)
* Extension west of Dalston Junction to Canonbury and Highbury & Islington (two stations)

Left: *Within New Cross Gate depot maintenance area on 28 June 2010 is No 378135, demonstrating how easy it is for fitters to get beneath the train to give it attention. The depot area aims to provide easy access to the stock at all the physical levels that might be needed by maintenance staff.* John Glover

* Extension south of Surrey Quays to Clapham Junction (six stations).

The timetable

So much perhaps for the theory – what does the timetable look like on the East London Line? That operated by Southern Railway immediately prior to the new service starting is shown in Table 17.3 (see p111). This is the Mondays to Fridays middle day, off-peak timetable, shown in terms of the minutes past the hour and in one direction only. Table 17.4 (see p111) shows the equivalent information from 23 May 2010 when the new services started.

Operators are London Overground (LO) and Southern (SN). Again, all trains shown call at all intermediate stations on the lines concerned. Note that only the trains from London Bridge that call intermediately between there and East/West Croydon are shown.

It will be noted that the number of Southern trains has reduced from six to four, and that there is now no service from London Bridge to West Croydon. On the other hand, West Croydon now receives four trains an hour instead of two, though all come from Dalston Junction. Crystal Palace sees its services rise from two to six, with the frequencies from London Bridge remaining the same. There is in effect no change to the East Croydon services.

Future services

All this activity has a substantial impact on the map of London's railways. This will result in a service frequency of at least 15 minutes on all sections other than Watford

Note that the services operated by Southern which run on a basically hourly headway on the West London Line but do not serve Willesden Junction, are excluded.

There are 4tph all day Monday to Saturdays from Gospel Oak to Barking, reducing to 2tph on Sundays. This latter is roundly double the prevalent service levels for many years.

The East London connection along the Broad Street viaduct became fully active in 2010, with 12tph all day and every day from the newly re-created Dalston Junction to Whitechapel, and a choice of three destinations further south of New Cross, West Croydon and Crystal Palace. The latter two were back-extended to Highbury & Islington when that section opened in 2011.

2012 services

This leaves the South London services to Clapham Junction, introduced in 2012. These provide the 'missing' 4tph in the East London core timetable between Dalston Junction and Surrey Quays, bringing services over this section up to 16tph. The Highbury & Islington section then sees 8tph beyond Dalston Junction, with 4tph service levels to each of the four branches in the south.

Thus these sections of line have a much better level of service than they have had in recent years, or in some instances perhaps better than they have ever had before.

This is for a post-Olympic timetable, which assumes further track work in the Camden Road area. The expenditure of £54 million has been approved, and this is intended to allow the freight tracks to be extended westwards from where they currently end in the vicinity of the North London connection to the Great Northern main line through to Camden Road Junction. Keeping freight and passenger traffic apart as far as possible is to the benefit of all operators concerned.

Above: It would seem that some care has been taken not to draw attention to the unfortunate coincidences, such as going downstairs from the Underground's District Line at Whitechapel to reach the Overground on the East London. But the train in this picture of 28 April 2010 is undoubtedly a D stock District Line train. John Glover

Junction-Euston, although the section between Harrow & Wealdstone and Queen's Park also has services provided by London Underground's Bakerloo Line. The National Rail timetable makes little reference to this other than the non-committal remark that 'Stations Harrow & Wealdstone to Queen's Park inclusive are also served by London Underground Bakerloo Line services'. So one arm of an organisation has its services in the timetable, the other hasn't. Competition? No, just the perpetuation of history. But it raises other issues, to be discussed.

Services will be operated generally by four-car electric trains, but with two-car diesel trains between Gospel Oak and Barking.

Looking at the May 2011 timetable, there is a 6tph all-day service, every day, between Stratford and Willesden Junction, increased to 8tph at peak. Of these, 4tph proceed to Richmond and 2tph to Clapham Junction. There are also an additional 2tph off peak between Willesden Junction and Clapham Junction only.

Right: This pair of units, Nos 378140/52, is in the main maintenance area at New Cross Gate depot on 28 June 2010. No third rail traction power is provided anywhere within the depot; trains arrive using their own momentum and depart by hitching up to a depot supply until they reach the live rail. John Glover

Above: An eastbound service for Stratford formed by No 378023 is seen at Camden Road on 29 June 2010. The large and capacious canopy on the right for passengers joining the westbound services is not replicated in any sense on the other platform. John Glover

Table 17.3: 13 December 2009 timetable Mondays to Fridays, off-peak, minutes past the hour

	SN	SN	SN	SN	SN	SN	SN
London Bridge	-	05	15	24	35	45	54
New Cross Gate	10	20	30	40	50	00	-
Sydenham	21	31	40	51	01	10	-
Crystal Palace	-	-	43	-	-	13	-
West Croydon	-	45	-	-	15	-	-
East Croydon	29	-	-	59	-	-	-

The operator throughout is Southern (SN). All trains shown call at all intermediate stations on the lines concerned.

Table 17.4: 23 May 2010 timetable Mondays to Fridays, middle day, off-peak, minutes past the hour

	LO	LO	SN	LO	LO	LO	SN	LO	LO	LO	SN	LO	LO	LO	SN	LO
London Bridge	-	-	22	-	-	-	36	-	-	-	52	-	-	-	06	-
Dalston Junction	00	05	-	10	15	20	-	25	30	35	-	40	45	50	-	55
Surrey Quays	17	22	-	27	32	37	-	42	47	52	-	57	02	07	-	12
New Cross	-	28	-	-	-	43	-	-	-	58	-	-	-	13	-	-
New Cross Gate	22	-	27	32	37	-	41	47	52	-	57	02	07	-	22	17
Sydenham	32	-	38	42	47	-	52	57	02	-	08	12	17	-	22	27
Crystal Palace	37	-	43	-	52	-	-	-	07	-	13	-	22	-	-	42
West Croydon	-	-	-	01	-	-	-	12	-	-	-	31	-	-	33	-
East Croydon	-	-	-	-	-	-	03	-	-	-	-	-	-	-	-	-

Operators: Southern (SN), London Overground (LO).

Above: *Being open for traffic does not necessarily mean that all work is finished. This is the view from the footbridge at Caledonian Road & Barnsbury, looking west on 4 June 2010, which emphasises the width of the new island platform.* John Glover

Right: *The new station at Caledonian Road & Barnsbury uses the two centre tracks around a new island platform, seen here on 4 June 2010 with No 378006 arriving from Stratford. The platform on the right is only useful as the station entrance/exit, since it has a fence to keep passengers away from the line. It is intended for use only by freight.* John Glover

Other train operators

London Overground is a substantial operator in its own right, but it does not operate all the stations at which it calls. This is generally the preserve of the operator with the most train calls at that station; details may be found in Appendix A, which lists all the stations in which London Overground has an interest, together with dates of opening and other details.

London Overground also shares the infrastructure with other operators. Most notably, this includes the District Line of London Underground between Gunnersbury and Richmond, and the Bakerloo Line between Queen's Park and Harrow & Wealdstone. A third possibility in which a similar situation could come about is if the Croxley link were built. Then the Metropolitan and the Watford DC lines would share tracks over the final stretch between Watford High Street and Watford Junction. Also, of course, the Bakerloo could once more be extended to Watford Junction. What is the future of the link to Euston?

As noted, Southern also shares extensive sections of infrastructure with London Overground. Other major sharers are the freight operators, which may appear almost anywhere on the national network. There are also trains run for engineering purposes.

Interchange

Passenger interchange with other services is perhaps less common than might be imagined; it is likely to take place at only about 20 of the stations in the London Overground 2012 portfolio.

This divides into interchange with other National Rail lines, with Underground lines, or with both. The proportions are around one-third each, and it may be that connections with other parts of the national system are in practice as valuable for London Overground users as those to the Underground.

There are also the stations where the nearest Underground is within a reasonable walking distance of (say) 500 metres, were one to exploit it. This is the situation at West Hampstead, Shepherds Bush and Camden Road.

Above: Surrey Quays station at platform level sees No 378141 arriving on a southbound service on 28 April 2010. Four-car trains have replaced four-car trains on the East London Line itself, so what is the difference? John Glover

Left: Changes to the 1980s Surrey Quays station have not affected the outside appearance, seen here as it was on 28 April 2010. The branding of course now reads London Overground. John Glover

CHAPTER 18: **WHO DOES WHAT?**

It is of interest to consider the physical sizes of the various rail transport providers in Greater London, as shown in Table 18.1. It may come as some surprise to find that Network Rail accounts for twice the total route distance of the Underground, but many of the former's routes from the 14 central London terminals diverge to serve several different corridors, and virtually all of them reach out beyond the Greater London boundary. By contrast, only a few Underground routes extend beyond fare Zone 5.

The national network is dominant south of the Thames, although the construction of the Jubilee Line extension raised the number of stations south of the river served by the Underground to 33.

Who should run them?

There is no easy answer to this question. Where services run entirely within the area of a city authority, there is much to be said for that authority taking control of the various aspects of planning and finance, and perhaps also operations. But if the operations spread out beyond that boundary, other factors become important.

Thus few would consider Transport for London as the most obvious body to control the West Coast Main Line to Glasgow. When it comes to the four stations beyond Headstone Lane that take the Watford DC lines into Hertfordshire, the answer is less certain. Do the people of Hertfordshire really want a body they don't elect to determine service provision in all

Fig 18.1: Rail transport providers in Greater London		
Operator	Route km	%
London Underground	392	31.7
Network Rail	788	63.8
London Tramlink	29	2.3
Docklands Light Railway	27	2.2
Totals	1,236	100.0
Source: Transport for London		

its detail, the type of trains that will run their services, and the fares they are charged? Or would they prefer a national body such as the Department for Transport to specify such matters?

For herein lies the problem. The very nature of National Rail operations is that they are in principle open to all-comers, and that includes freight, local passenger, commuter and long-distance passenger alike. They may meet national, regional or local needs or, as in most stretches of railway, some combination. They also form a network, in that the number of available routes and the capacity of each are by definition also limited. Thus where capacity is in short supply there has to be some form of priority in the granting of access rights by Network Rail.

What realistic alternatives are available to resolve such conflicts? Occasionally single-purpose lines can be defined, but it is perhaps undesirable for an infrastructure controller to be responsible to local interests.

Right: Proposals for the CrossLink service were to make considerable use of the North London Line, though only the initial service ever materialised. Here, Anglia-liveried No 170202 approaches South Acton with the 12:32 Basingstoke to Chelmsford service in May 2001. It is on the otherwise freight-only line from Kew Bridge and, as can be seen, the route of the electric services to Richmond curves sharply to the left.
John Glover

Service frequencies

On the East London, 'Customers will benefit from new walk-through air-conditioned trains, four newly built stations and 14 refurbished stations with upgraded CCTV, passenger information systems and lighting with staff on duty at all times while trains are running. The route will provide a turn up and go, metro-style service of up to (initially) 12 trains an hour to parts of London traditionally poorly served by rail services.'

The use of a 'turn-up-and-go' service level is interesting. Does that mean that public timetables will become superfluous? That they need not even be produced? That is, after all, the position on London Underground; there are detailed departure sheets giving service intervals, times of first and last trains and journey time predictions, and these are freely available. Provided that the service is frequent enough, and there is certainly room for debate as to what frequency that might be, it is the regularity of the service that is of most interest to the passenger. More detailed enquiries can be made on the web or by phone.

Compare that with National Rail, where the timetable of the 1970s had its page size all but halved, then more recently halved again. The size of the type face followed suit, making it less than a joy to read. At the same time, the National Rail timetable for the second half of 2011 managed still to consist of 3,264 pages; that for 1979/80 lasted a year and told all in 1,336 pages.

Telling the public

How then can train services best be advised to the public? The author was intrigued to hear a complaint that the 'next train' indicators on the East London give the timetabled time of a train, then its expected arrival time. 'Why not just "next train 3 mins", then reducing, as on the Underground?' he asked. That, it seemed, was one of the results of being part of the National Rail system, with which operators like LOROL have to fit in.

The whole perhaps reveals a different approach to train running. On the national system punctuality and reliability – which dropped a decade ago to dreadful levels – have become something of a Holy Grail in the way that operator performance is measured, publicised and penalised for failure. On urban Metro-type services, different criteria apply, with service regularity being of high importance. That also helps keep to platforms clear and avoid overcrowding.

If trains appear regularly at five-minute (or whatever) intervals as promised, does it matter to the passenger if they are all a quarter of an hour late?

Yet London Overground has to contend with other operators on the same tracks, where line capacity may be a prime requirement. This is considered further in the next section, and later in terms of what Network Rail's various Route Utilisation Strategies have had to say.

Open access

The developments on the North London railway show what can be done to maximise its use through regulation of who can use it and when. The juxtaposition of heavy freight and modest-sized passenger trains is not ideal, and can only be taken so far before a whole new tranche of investment is required. That could even require a new railway to be constructed, the implications of which in a fully built-up area are huge. That is quite apart from the costs of so doing, and deciding how these are to be met.

The provision of non-franchised open access services was one of the rallying points of the Conservative Government that introduced the

Above: *Open access has not been a major force on National Rail, but that could always change; the necessary legislation is in place. Here, open access operator Wrexham & Shropshire runs a service between Marylebone and Wrexham. With Driving Van Trailer No 82325 leading and a Class 67 locomotive at the rear providing power, the ensemble of Mk III coaches passes the Underground station at Neasden on 29 April 2009. These services ceased less than a year later.* John Glover

Right: *Freightliner is a heavy user of the North London Line, and here Class 86s double-head a train through Stratford Regional station towards the East Coast ports on 4 April 2008, with No 86604 leading. These locomotives are well on their way to achieving half a century of service, having been built in quantity for West Coast Main Line work in the mid-1960s.*
John Glover

Below: *There is nothing new about the acquiring of the infrastructure of other railways by new operators, together often with substantial investment. Thus the Northern Line extension to High Barnet of 1940 was designed to help the LNER in wrestling with its suburban problem and offer a whole new range of destinations for passengers. Seen here is the southbound platform at Totteridge & Whetstone station on 29 June 2008, with a special train of polished 1938 tube stock, though it will not stop. These were the original Underground trains to be used here, superseding the LNER Class N2 0-6-2Ts which thereafter were used on the freight traffic until that ceased.* John Glover

privatisation of the national system with the Railways Act 1993. Few took it up, and they met with mixed success. In any event, it did not fit with the planned economy approach under Labour. This is an illustration of what open access meant in the case of London CrossLink, a service that ran from 30 May 2000 to 11 September 2002.

GB Railways

GB Railways was the operator of the then Anglia franchise, which covered broadly those parts of East Anglia not part of the former Network SouthEast, plus the former Norwich–Liverpool Street InterCity service. The company saw an opportunity for a package of new train services to link the railway networks north and south of London that could be run commercially without taxpayer support and offer many new journey opportunities. The cross-London services were identified as:

* Ipswich-Watford, with a possible extension to Northampton
* Ipswich-Basingstoke
* Watford-Basingstoke

They would be marketed under the name of London CrossLink. All would be provided with air-conditioned rolling stock, relieve road congestion and make travelling easier for those who found use of the Underground a trial. It will be appreciated that all the services required the use of the North or West London lines.

In the event, the only service to be operated was that between (as it turned out) Norwich and Basingstoke. Initially, the calling points were Diss, Stowmarket, Ipswich, Colchester, Witham, Chelmsford, Romford, Stratford, Highbury & Islington, West Hampstead, Feltham, Staines, Woking and Farnborough Main. There were six trains each way on weekdays and five on Sundays.

That, however, was the good news; the reality was more prosaic, as Table 18.2 shows. There are several curious features about this timetable, but regular-interval it was not. One feature that is not apparent from this extract is that it was only possible to get back to Stowmarket or Diss on a Sunday, when there was a choice of two services. There was no service back to Romford at all.

Much of the difficulty was no doubt caused by the inability to obtain train paths at the times desired, but it does illustrate the inter-related problems. Services of this nature need a path for the throughout journey; it is of little value if the problem can be solved on the North London (say), but meets with intractable constraints on the Great Eastern or South Western.

New calling patterns emerged, and Camden Road and Brentford both appeared in the final timetable, but London CrossLink did not survive after 28 September 2002. Maybe there will be encouragement again for open access operators in the future, but the train path conundrum still has to be solved.

High Speed 2

There are huge benefits that Britain could derive from a new high-speed railway if one was built between London Euston, Birmingham and the North, but only one aspect need detain us here. That is the proposal by the HS2 team to introduce a second 'London' station on railway land at Old Oak Common, in the Acton area.

This is a large site, bigger than the Stratford railway lands, which were always considered substantial in their own right. It is situated in an area bounded to the south by the Great Western main line, and to the west by the North London Line (and also the Dudding Hill line of the Midland) and, a little further away, by London Underground's Central Line. To the east there is the West London Line, and to the north the Willesden Junction complex. The Paddington branch of the Grand Union Canal threads its way through the whole, broadly between the south-east and the north-west, which means that some of the land to its north is filled by an industrial estate.

If an Old Oak Common station on HS2 was to be built, it would need above all good public transport access. This could be achieved in a number of ways, the basis of which would be a station on Crossrail, which would have the benefit of frequent rail services to the Paddington, Bond Street, Moorgate/Liverpool Street and Canary Wharf areas, thus offsetting the limitations of Euston as the terminus. Services to West London and beyond would also be provided.

It would also be an ideal point from which to reach the various Heathrow terminals from a development of the 'Heathrow Express' service. The problem of a single 'Heathrow' station is that it cannot serve all the existing terminals, and a second means of transit will be necessary for at least some of them. From Old Oak Common it is possible to serve all of them.

Old Oak and the Overground

From the point of view of HS2 passengers from the north or south, use of the Overground services would be made simple by placing a new station on each of the North and West London lines as close to the Old Oak Common station as could be arranged. The destinations to be reached do not need repetition here, except perhaps to remind readers of the vast further number of destinations that could be reached by a single change of train at Clapham Junction.

A further possibility is the use of the now disused North Pole Eurostar depot area to accommodate further terminating platforms. This could bring large numbers of additional passengers to London Overground lines, which might or might not be welcomed in terms of the extra strains they would put on the then existing passenger services. On the whole, the problems of growth are more amenable to management action than those of decline; at least in the case of growth there is income to help pay for the works required.

The Crossrail project itself will also serve Stratford, though this seems unlikely to have much direct material effect on London Overground services. To the extent that it helps regenerate the area, though, employment and travel to work may both increase, and that will also generate traffic to be accommodated somehow.

Rail Strategy for London

The pressures on the transport providers in London are not likely to ease, with the population likely to rise to 8 million by 2026. Hence the warning in TfL's Rail Strategy of 2007, that the combination of concentrated employment growth in a few areas and dispersed housing growth across inner and Greater London, as well as the wider South East, will increase the already large commuting task.

Table 18.2: East Anglia-Basingstoke timetable, Anglia Railways, Mondays to Fridays, 28 May-23 September 2000						
Norwich				09 34		
Diss				09 43		
Stowmarket				09 55		
Ipswich	04 40			10 07		
Colchester	05 00		08 38	10 27		
Witham				10 46	13 25	
Chelmsford	05 18		08 59	10 55	13 35	15 22
Romford	05 37					
Stratford	05 46		09 31	11 24	14 04	15 47
Highbury & Islington	05 57	08 18	09 44	11 43	14 21	16 01
West Hampstead	06 10	08 28	10 00	11 58	14 35	16 16
Feltham	06 37	09 06	10 36	12 31	15 06	16 51
Staines	06 43	09 12	10 41	12 39	15 12	16 57
Woking	07 10	09 40	11 14	13 00	15 36	17 23
Farnborough (Main)				13 11	15 51	
Basingstoke	07 31	10 00	11 35	13 28	16 04	17 45

Above: *Richmond is a South West Trains station, as the branding in this view of 12 September 2009 clearly indicates, but it has to cope with the use of the premises by both London Underground and London Overground. How do the secondary operators ensure that their presence is known to the general public, or is this not really important in the interests of co-ordinated service delivery?*
John Glover

Right: No 313104 leaves South Acton for Richmond in May 2001. Today, this modest station is the only one on the main North London Line to be equipped with just third rail electrification. It thus remains without the various paraphernalia associated with overhead line equipment. John Glover

Below: At Kenton, the fourtrack West Coast Main Line, with 25kV AC electrification, runs right next to what is in effect a separate railway carrying the DC lines. These are being used here by a Bakerloo Line train of Underground 1972 Mk 2 stock bound for Elephant & Castle. These tracks are electrified on the fourth rail principle. Such installations carry the benefit of grandfather rights ('it has always been like this'), but the extent to which any new construction on similar lines would be permitted is perhaps becoming more doubtful. The date is 27 October 1998. John Glover

Transport for London's own projections (as part of its Transport 2025 work) suggest that rail passenger demand will increase over the next twenty years by 30-40%. Even if this is only in the right order of magnitude, the currently planned and funded rail projects will prove insufficient. That means crowding is going to get a whole deal worse, with many trains in the peak hour experiencing four people standing per square metre as trains approach the terminals. Think about it: that is a 500mm space each way to stand in, where you have roundly four times as much area for yourself today.

Is it possible? Yes, in the sense that anything is, but station closures to keep the premises safe will become commonplace. Around a dozen stations have been identified for high-priority treatment, and medium priority extends to a further 15. Note too that these are all National Rail stations; the Underground is another story.

Pricing

Pricing might make more of a contribution than it does at the moment, but off-peak fare reductions have been around for many years. TfL believes that demand management techniques are not going to be anything like enough to combat the problem. Neither is it a position in which we want to be; transport in a city is not based entirely on the financial benefits from fares. There is the value added to the areas served, and these economic benefits are captured by governments as well as private interests. Without effective action, there is a risk of an imbalance of prosperity. There will be more social exclusion and more pollution. The central objective is to increase efficiency and quality so as to create a world-class transport system for the capital.

The London Overground development has made a good start in these directions, but more is needed. For instance:

* The reconfiguration of rolling stock to provide more internal capacity with standing room, enabling increased loadings per train
* More vehicles per train, requiring the procurement of additional rolling stock, the lengthening of some platforms, signalling and track alterations to match, and work at maintenance areas and depots to provide accommodation
* An increase in train frequencies, which deliver large benefits to passengers but at some expense as it also requires more rolling stock, more track capacity,

signalling adjustments and, at least potentially, implications for service reliability
* Site-specific schemes for stations to provide capacity relief and to complement the greater numbers travelling.

TfL believes that it is possible to devise a range of schemes that together will meet the overall need in London and the South East. The single most effective scheme is Crossrail from Maidenhead and Heathrow to Shenfield and Abbey Wood. Now under construction, this will provide a step-change in capacity to support job growth in central London and the Isle of Dogs. It will promote the development of new areas such as the Thames Gateway and provide major congestion relief on the Underground.

Thameslink is the next element, again under construction, to provide north/south route relief. Again, this features longer trains and higher frequencies, and removes some of the need for commuters to transfer to the Underground to complete their journeys.

TfL's third element is the comprehensive upgrade of Waterloo, to allow longer trains to operate on the dense and heavily crowded lines from that terminus.

Mayor's wish list

Then there is a package of individual, relatively straightforward and cost-effective measures that the Mayor would like to see, including:

* Longer trains and platforms on West Anglia services and, later, increasing the number of tracks from two to four on the Lea Valley between Tottenham Hale and Cheshunt
* Longer trains and, where necessary, platform lengthening on Southern and Southeastern
* Provision of increased frequencies on the newly established London Overground services
* Conversion of the Watford-Euston DC lines to the Bakerloo Line between Queen's Park and Watford Junction. This is described elsewhere as the conversion of the Harrow & Wealdstone to Watford Junction section to Bakerloo Line operation. Quite what might be intended between Queen's Park and London Euston is not stated, but Network Rail sources suggest that the service might be rerouted via Primrose Hill to Stratford
* Purchase of additional rolling stock and/or reconfiguration and refurbishment of existing stock to make the best use of infrastructure on London Midland, Essex Thames-side and South West Trains
* Train Operating Company franchises – costed options including improved service frequencies across London so that service frequency of 4tph operates on most TOCs
* Smaller-scale schemes to make improvements to station security, accessibility and ambience.

It is suggested that the timing of such work should aim at minimising peaks in infrastructure and rolling

stock spending, and that the expected levels of overcrowding on each route should drive the order in which work proceeds. Matters like value for money and affordability appear as usual, as does ease of delivery. There is also the matter of how advanced each project might be.

Funding

What the document does stress, though, is that there is no long-term funded programme for London's railways as a whole, despite their importance to the economy and their passengers alike. 'Subsidy is less than 1p per passenger mile, while regional Train Operating Companies receive closer to 10p.'

The Strategy concludes, 'Given the scale of the transport task they face, railways are the poor relation of transport in London. Improvements in London's rail system are more necessary than anywhere else.'

The £1 billion investment in London Overground's new East London route was the biggest piece of

Above: There are opportunities to do much more at West Hampstead. These are the Jubilee Line platforms in August 2004, but is there an opportunity for additional platforms on the tracks used by Chiltern Railways on the far side? (The intermediate track is used by Metropolitan northbound services.) The London Overground station lies on the other side of West End Lane, which is the road on the overbridge, and the Thameslink station is a little further along the same road (to the right in this view). John Glover

Left: At Whitechapel, the District and Hammersmith & City lines pass over those of London Overground, which lies beneath the bridge girders in the middle distance. A D stock train is bound for Upminster in this April 1998 view. The East London Line here occupies a revamp of the pre-existing railway, but the potential disruption to be caused by the creation of new deeplevel platforms for Crossrail will put new strains on what is essentially old infrastructure. John Glover

Above: *Leytonstone High Road station is a long walk from the road from which this photograph was taken on 12 April 2010, and there is then a good flight of steps to climb. Are we really trying hard enough to make the railway an attractive proposition for shorter distance journeys? Faced with this and similar conditions at the other end of the journey, who could blame a potential passenger for thinking that catching a bus might be so much easier?* John Glover

transport infrastructure for London since the opening of the Jubilee Line extension in 1999. It was delivered ahead of schedule and on budget.

Public finances

In circumstances where public financing is less than buoyant, how can large-scale improvement schemes be funded? How, in other words, can private investors be repaid?

One of the biggest single risks is future ridership. While train operators can offer a service that meets all the quality tests, they have only a limited ability to influence ridership levels and hence revenue. This may be for activities several years in advance of when the investment is required. Thus, if economic activity falls, journeys to work will lessen, and this is not the fault of the operator. Similarly, if a booming economy causes them to rise, more passengers will be presenting themselves.

Thus, as an incentive to the private sector, government can offer some level of support to ridership levels, by capping the level of risk at, say, 80%. Or the government might pay the operator for each additional passenger journey made above a set figure.

Other risks are ensuring an effective construction management system, the use of the right technology and getting performance levels right, financing issues that need to be realistic in their approach to foreign exchange, interest rates and taxation, and the problems of obtaining planning permission.

Who should take these risks? No single solution applies everywhere, but there is a need to make the most of private sector involvement. Rail work is unlikely to be financed from fares revenue alone. The other risks cannot be ignored.

To attract private sector money, a risk-management-based solution is highly desirable. There are some things that will stay with government as the only body that can reasonably address them.

Moving forward

Where does all that leave us in respect of further advances? A major piece of work, or rather works, are the Route Utilisation Strategies (RUS) produced by Network Rail. These are individual strategies at line-of-route level, within the framework provided by the Capacity Utilisation Policy.

The aim is to provide properly performing train services that accommodate aspirations for growth in a way that maximises the value for money and is affordable. The Strategies focus on the short to medium term (three to ten years) of railway service provision, and on corridors where network capacity is constrained and there is a pressure for further development.

Those relevant to the area under consideration relate to Cross-London movements, the North London RUS

Right: *Stepping distances, both vertical and horizontal, can be a problem for all sorts of users, notably small children and the elderly. This is Ewell West on 4 September 2009, showing the difference in height to be negotiated when boarding or leaving a South West Trains Class 455 unit. Do we need to do better, and how does expenditure on such issues, which are hardly of recent origin, compare with other spending priorities?* John Glover

and the South London RUS. These have the considerable benefit of making reference to the railway network as a whole, without what is essentially the artificial limitation of political boundaries. The problem of the latter is that political regimes tend to look inward. If they do consider matters outside their own boundaries, actions that they might take will be evaluated primarily in terms of the benefits (or otherwise) to those within. These are, after all, the people who vote them into office; those outside have no such ability.

Tensions

This is intended as a general comment, but there are real tensions in such situations. Does what works for shorter-distance passengers work equally well for those covering longer distances? This includes matters such as the ratio of seats to standing spaces in trains, the importance or otherwise of multiple doors to reduce station dwell times, the frequency of stops and

where they are made, and so on. They will all vary. Train operating companies will also point out that the longer-distance passengers provide much more revenue per journey, so they are perhaps entitled to a higher degree of service.

Much of this is down to the TOCs to provide in relation to what they judge to be in their best commercial interests, within the requirements of the terms of their franchises. Very little of the national railway network is contained wholly within even as large a geographical area as Greater London; even the stations from Carpenders Park to Watford Junction as served by London Overground are actually in Hertfordshire.

There is always a compromise to be made in such matters and a balance to be struck between the interested parties. On the national system, that includes freight interests too. Where there are only two tracks available over long stretches, as on the North London Line, the difficulties can become intense.

Above: Unit No 172001 leaves Upper Holloway station for Barking on 19 August 2011. As with many others on this line, this station has undergone extensive refurbishment, and the long ramp from the street to the platform can be seen in the background. All stations on this line are now staffed and have a ticket office. John Glover

Left: The former site of Willesden Junction main-line platforms on 12 September 2009 sees London Midland No 350104 hurrying north. The link to the West London Line is out of the picture to the right, but any platforms reinstated there would be a very long way from any other passenger facilities. John Glover

CHAPTER 19: **FUTURE CHALLENGES**

Above: The line to Crystal Palace diverges from that to Norwood Junction south of Sydenham station with the use of a flying junction. By the time it reaches Penge West it is on a substantial viaduct, seen here from outside the latter station on 12 April 2010. The need for infrastructure of this magnitude depends substantially on the lie of the land, but its continued maintenance remains a long-term cost for the railway undertakings. John Glover

The biggest single challenge facing the railway today would seem to be that of line capacity. Nowhere is this more acute than on the North London Line, which has a mix of passenger services which have already been described, and freight traffic.

Freight

Freight services are operated by a full range of operators in that field. Their volume is best expressed in terms of trains per 24hr, and excepting the East London and the DC lines, all the routes used by London Overground have heavy freight usage. Apart from services related to ports, including Tilbury, the routes see significant volumes to local terminals and yards in and around London, including aggregates and sand. There are also bulk commodities such as waste, automotive, petroleum, Ministry of Defence traffic and (for a period) Olympics construction. There are also some LUL infrastructure service trains which access that system at Barking or Gunnersbury.

Origins and destinations vary widely, which means that freights join and leave the passenger lines at a number of junctions on routes which do not normally carry passenger services. However, the core section of the North London between Camden Road and Gospel Oak presently sees about 40 freights a day.

Generally, routes are cleared for running at up to 45mph but there are sections, particularly around Willesden, where 35mph or less is the norm. Route availability and gauge enhancement works for freight have made substantial improvements in recent times.

It will be appreciated that both passenger and freight traffic are expected to grow substantially in the years to come, but can they all be accommodated?

North London core

The key central section of the North London line is that between Camden Road and Dalston, a distance of about three miles.

From the west at Camden Road, the line via Hampstead Heath is joined by that from Primrose Hill on the West Coast Main Line. There then follows a short section of double track until Camden Road East Junction is reached. From here, the single track electrified link to the East Coast Main Line and the connection into High Speed 1 to St Pancras and to Stratford International diverges on the Down side. Also from here, the North London line expands to a four-track formation.

The new pattern of services has seen trains (now from the East London Line) reinstated over the Dalston Western Curve over a section of line now dedicated to their use to Canonbury and Highbury & Islington, terminating there in the two platforms on the south side of the formation.

Between Camden Road East Junction and Dalston Western Junction, the four tracks have had their use and directional priorities changed. From north to south of the formation, the former Down North London No.1 Line has become the Down North London Relief Line, but essentially retains its use for freight services. The former Up North London No.1 Line has become the Down NLL and is used for both passenger and freight.

The former Down North London No.2 Line has become a bi-directional Up North London Reversible Line used by both passenger and freight, and the former Up North London No.2 Line has become the Up NLL and is now used exclusively for freight services. On this section of line is Caledonian Road & Barnsbury station, which used to have two platforms either side of the No.2 Lines, but now has an island platform between the Up North London Reversible Line and the Down NLL.

The whole of the NLL on this section is electrified at 25kV AC, and this continues over the section where all four lines converge into the Up and Down NLL as they reach Highbury & Islington station. The other two platforms carrying the East London Line services are electrified at 750v DC.

The Down ELL has a short transfer line onto the NLL and the Up ELL is now a terminal track.

National system

Most of the routes under consideration in this book are part of the national railway system, the continued well-being of which is the direct concern of Network Rail as its custodian. (The East London Line and its extensions to Dalston and towards Old Kent Road

Junction are the exceptions, being vested in Transport for London.) Thus the system has to meet today's needs, but also those of the future.

Network Rail has developed a system of Route Utilisation Strategies (RUS) in which the company sets out its thoughts and proposals for future action. These start life as consultation documents, to be revised and confirmed later. Those relevant to the areas under discussion are outlined below.

Cross-London RUS

'Historically, the Cross-London lines have been seen as strategic freight routes, but fast-rising passenger demand is forcing the industry to review this status.' John Armitt, the then Chief Executive of Network Rail, in his Foreword to the Cross-London Route Utilisation Strategy.

Much of what was contained in this RUS which dates from 2006 has already been committed or actually carried out. The present discussion also takes into account Network Rail's 2011 Network Specifications. That for the North London line includes the Tottenham & Hampstead and the Dudding Hill line, and associated connections to all London's main radial routes. It also takes account of the Freight RUS, published in 2007.

These lines are referred to collectively in this section as the North London group.

The context is set out clearly. 'The North London group is a vital part of London's transport infrastructure and a major link between key arterial routes to and from the capital. It is a nationally important freight route and provides a key passenger service around London, with connections to/from every arterial route north, east and west of London.' To that might be added south of London too, via the West London line.

It adds that the Eastern Regional Planning Assessment suggests that there will be continuing growth in commuting to the centre of London and Docklands. 'However, parts of the current North London route are already operating at or close to capacity in terms of train paths.'

Current demands

The North London group serves local communities and provides both journey to work as well as all day business, leisure and shopping travel. There is some competition with other forms of transport, but mostly rail has the fastest journey time. Demand is being driven by increasing employment and population in many of the areas served.

Above: *The terminal platforms used for the London Overground suburban services at Euston (Nos 9 and 10, seen here on 26 March 2010) are rather shorter than most. They are also the only ones equipped for DC traction. What will happen to them in the long term both while Euston rebuilding is undertaken and subsequently? Will or should the DC services be diverted elsewhere, and what alternative facilities can be offered to South Hampstead and Kilburn High Road?* John Glover

Left: *Sometimes heavy rail and the Underground run in parallel, as seen here south of Stratford Market in October 2001. On the left is the Jubilee Line and on the right what was the North Woolwich branch. In between it was deemed necessary to erect this substantial barrier. Now that the National Rail branch has been converted to Docklands Light Railway operation, does the same requirement hold good? Separations of this sort are fine, provided that space permits.* John Glover

FUTURE CHALLENGES

Right: *At Leyton Midland Road passengers have a long flight of steps to negotiate to and from the platforms. How does the railway ensure that it is worth their while to do so? Should they choose not to, there is no fares income and ultimately no railway. The date is 13 April 2010.* John Glover

Far right: *Signal heads using LEDs (light-emitting diodes) are now becoming commonplace in railway use; this one is at the western end of Dalston Kingsland platforms on 10 April 2010 and indicates that the train will be taking the left-hand branch (No 2 line and DC third rail only). Drivers of electric trains are reminded to lower pantographs. All this has now changed, and straight on is the only (25kV AC) option.* John Glover

The main rail passenger interchanges are:

* Stratford, for Central and Jubilee lines, Docklands
  Light Railway and Abellio East Anglia services.
* Highbury & Islington for East London line, Great
  Northern suburban and Victoria lines.
* West Hampstead, for Jubilee line and Thameslink,
  both nearby.
* Willesden Junction, for Bakerloo and London
  Overground Watford dc lines.
* Gunnersbury, for District line.
* Richmond, for South West Trains.
* Barking, for Essex Thames-side, Hammersmith &
  City and District lines.
* Blackhorse Road, for Victoria line.
* Gospel Oak, between London Overground lines.

There are no passenger services on the Dudding Hill line.

Stratford is the gateway to Docklands, where employment is expanding as well as at the new Stratford City development. There is also interchange with High Speed 1 and the domestic services operated by Southeastern.

Freight demand, especially intermodal from the Port of Felixstowe, is growing by 4%-5% a year. This is likely to increase further with new port developments at Felixstowe South and Bathside Bay, Harwich, when these come on stream. Such trains will approach on the Great Eastern main line. There is also the deep sea London Gateway Port at Shellhaven, whose traffic will approach via Barking.

Forecasts show that Felixstowe could generate an additional 26 trains per day over and above 2004/05 base year levels, but down to 18 when the London Gateway Port is developed. That alone could originate up to as many as 30 trains a day by 2030.

There is increasing demand for train paths over the North London group of lines as a whole.

Capacity issues

'The whole of the North London group is governed by the mixture of stopping passenger and through running freight service, complex junctions and station occupancy. These issues are often interlinked and overall route capacity is constrained by a combination of these factors. Key issues on the route are:

* Current and future levels of both passenger and
  freight services.
* Lack of alternative electrified route for freight traffic
  from Thames-side away from the Great Eastern
  route via Forest Gate and Stratford.
* Long signalling headways and the large number of
  junctions.
* Weight restrictions for freight trains on the
  Tottenham & Hampstead.
* Constraints on westbound services from Thames-
  side across Gospel Oak Junction.
* Passenger overcrowding at a number of stations
  including Blackhorse Road, Dalston Kingsland,
  Highbury & Islington and Homerton at peak times,
  and high levels of transfers to and from other
  services.

All passenger trains stop at all stations, where they interact with through freights. As a result, most of the route is operating close to track capacity for most of the day, so that any problem will cause a knock on effect on following services. This can quickly cause large amounts of reactionary delay from what might initially have been a small incident.

The main performance problems affecting Network Rail in recent times have been broken rails and track faults, points failures, track circuit failures, trespass and vegetation obstructing the infrastructure.

Station spacing

The spacing between stations is very variable and history usually has much to with it. However, as a basic proposition, the greater the number of intermediate stops, the slower the overall journey time. That makes the journey rather less attractive for the relatively longer distance passenger, though it favours the short distance.

This begs the question of for whom the railway is run. Railways thrive on volume, and are very good at carrying large numbers of people over longer distances. The more stops they make, the second advantage is at least diminished. That is all right up to a point, but they do need to remain sufficiently attractive to encourage those travelling longer distances.

Table 19.1 shows some statistics for the main groups of services which go to make up London Overground services in 2012. This shows the overall length of each line, the number of stations served, the average distance between stations and the average journey speed.

It is immediately apparent from the Table that the Euston to Watford Junction service returns the fastest journeys at 22.6 mph, with stations a fraction under one mile apart. This is probably due to its having been

Above: *Freight traffic is a major component of North London Line traffic. No 59202 emerges from Hampstead Heath Tunnel at Finchley Road & Frognal with a westbound train of stone empties on 10 February 2010. Passenger comforts are sparse at a station that used to sport covered staircases and long platform canopies. What should be the provision standards for lesser used urban stations such as these? John Glover*

Table 19.1: Physical characteristics of London Overground lines, 2010				
Line	Length	Stations	Inter-station distances	Average journey speed
London Euston to Watford Junction	17m 56ch	19	0m 79ch	22.6 mph
Gospel Oak to Barking	11m 78ch	12	1m 07ch	21.2 mph
Clapham Junction to Willesden Junction	6m 35ch	6	1m 23ch	17.6 mph
Richmond to Stratford	17m 50ch	23	0m 64ch	16.8 mph
Dalston Junction to West Croydon	13m 12ch	19	0m 58ch	15.5 mph

All distances are shown in miles and chains (80 chains to one mile), as this is still used for the national rail system of which all these services are part. Further details are shown in Appendix B.

FUTURE CHALLENGES

Above: *West Croydon station entrance shows distinct signs of Southern Railway concrete construction on 12 April 2010, but the premises themselves are some of the less appealing on the London Overground network. There is much to be done here.* John Glover

laid out as an entity designed for suburban running with electric traction, and with very little other traffic to contend with other than the joint operation with the Bakerloo line over the central section.

Perhaps surprisingly, the Gospel Oak to Barking service comes a close second. Here the stations are slightly more widely spaced and the diesel traction will have less good acceleration powers than an electric train, but 21.2 mph seems commendable.

Speed restrictions

The Clapham Junction to Willesden Junction service is plagued by severe speed restrictions at both ends of the journey, a single platform only at the southern end, and the stop for AC/DC changeover purposes. It also runs on a busy part of the network, which limits the availability of timetable slots. Nevertheless, an average of 17.6 mph is reasonable in the circumstances.

Then we get to the long established electric service from Richmond, nowadays to Stratford rather than Broad Street. The end-to-end journey takes 63 minutes for 17m 50ch, at a 16.8 mph average speed. The timing compares unfavourably with the only very slightly shorter distance from Euston to Watford Junction, which is accomplished in only 47 mins. Heavy traffic, mostly freight, has to be accommodated, and this is in no sense a line designed for speedy running.

The new line

Finally, there is the new line in the pack, Dalston Junction to West Croydon. Covering 13m 12ch in 51 mins gives a doleful 15.5 mph average over 19 stations. This is however a situation where averages can be deceptive. Analysis shows that in the 4m 26ch between Dalston Junction and Surrey Quays, these trains call at eight intermediate stations. None of these are more than 58 chains apart, and the closest are Canada Water and Rotherhithe. Here, the inter-station distance is 17 chains only, rather less than a quarter of a mile. Further south

the distances widen out to something closer to one mile, apart from Penge West to Anerley at 32 chains.

Overall, perhaps the main lesson is that while buses might cope well or at least reasonably well with shorter distance traffic, there is little alternative to rail for the longer journeys. Rail planners must therefore ensure that these longer distance flows do not get forgotten in the rush to satisfy the short distance market. It is a little sad but also true that there any number of people who will support suggestions for additional stations.

A policy which also seeks to remove those whose usage is insufficient to earn their keep and which slow the whole operation down to the detriment of passengers and operators alike, will never have any popular appeal.

Future demand

Peak passenger demand is expected to increase by 1%-1.5% a year across the route, and faster into Stratford. The latter is also now a focal point for journeys to London City Airport (via the DLR) as well as HS1. There is also the transient but highly important demand for access to the London games in 2012. Other factors seen as most likely to influence demand are developments in Docklands, interchange with the East London line and the continued expansion of the East Coast ports.

Capacity works to accommodate the expanded London Overground services have already been detailed. Network Rail believes that the solution to passenger growth and future capacity requirements can be met by a combination of the following:

* Longer trains, supported by platform lengthening and other rolling stock changes, which will need a complete review of the available traction power supply.
* Incremental introduction of additional services.
* Incremental enhancements delivered as improvements to planned track and signalling renewals, together with stand alone enhancements. These will improve performance, which is necessary for growth, enable increases in train paths, and facilitate timetable restructuring.
* Provision of additional passenger capacity and facilities at key stations.

A further problem in the Camden Road area where the railway is on brick arches will be the effect of the proposed link between High Speed 2 and High Speed 1. This is to run from Primrose Hill, through Camden Road station, and thence to the existing connection to HS1 where it diverges at Camden Road East. This would enable the provision of direct services from the Midlands and the north to Europe, with perhaps two trains per hour.

How can this best be accommodated over a distance of about a mile on or alongside the North London?

Left: *There are always other railway users not related to the incumbent operators to be accommodated from time to time. Here No 165110 of First Great Western heads west through Kensal Rise on 15 April 2010. Volumes of other traffic of this nature are often unpredictable, but the combination of available train paths and the reasonable requirements of other parties are one of the constraints in a national railway system.* John Glover

Predictions and actual results

There is of course the caveat that all the above are predictions. Fortunately, any operational problems faced by London Overground on the East London line or in its interactions with Southern services are not transmitted to the North London line. They are kept physically separate. How reliable will the new passenger rolling stock prove to be? How will passenger numbers turn out in reality? Will freight growth proceed as predicted?

While this discussion has centred around the North London group of lines, equally important for much of the freight traffic is what happens on the main radial routes which it also traverses. Can the very tight train path allocations on the North London group be allowed to determine the previous or subsequent freight train paths on the Great Eastern and West Coast main lines, for instance?

The answer is 'no', but with caution. The aim is to get the best possible result for the railway as a whole, and some nuts are easier to crack than others. The extended flat junctions between Forest Gate and Stratford used by long and relatively slow freights are an operator's nightmare, and if such a train has to come to a stop on them it will take a lot more time to get it going again. Therefore, this has to be avoided, like the plague. This theme is taken up by the East Anglia Route Plan.

But such are the joys and penalties of operating a mixed-traffic railway.

FUTURE CHALLENGES

Above: *Railway engineering work is an expensive business, so what can be done to bring unit costs down? This appears to be a busy scene at Highbury & Islington on Monday 28 June 2010 but, although it is not evident in a still photograph, it seemed that absolutely nothing at all was happening.* John Glover

Right: *South Bermondsey station is not part of London Overground (quite), but the problems here are not unusual in South London. How does this view strike the average person as an entrance to what amounts to a public utility? The television screen will provide some information and perhaps encourage you to go up the stairs, but is this the best the industry can do?* John Glover

Anglia

The capacity on the Great Eastern main line between Shenfield and Colchester is limited by a mix of fast and stopping passenger services on two tracks; this is further constrained by freight services. A combination of complex junctions, station occupancy and single line sections (elsewhere) make such issues worse. There is also a very heavy passenger peak.

The key issues are:
* The lack of an alternative route from the East Coast ports to the West Coast main line beyond Peterborough with W9 and W10 loading gauge capacity to relieve the Great Eastern main line of intermodal traffic.
* The freight from Thames-side using the GEML to reach the North London via Forest Gate Junction and Stratford.
* The lack of ability to recess freights on the GEML.
* Performance and congestion risks due to heavy line occupation.

These are not the only problems, but the above are mentioned here to show that what is perceived as a problem on the North London lines cannot be solved in isolation. Housing growth brings more commuting journeys, the need for 12-car trains and platform lengthening.

For freight it brings 640m or even longer trains, operating six days a week.

Containers

There are chilling words about container traffic. 'The use of 9ft 6in high containers continues to increase. Until 2008, the primary route for W10 gauge freight traffic was along the GEML from the east coast ports via Ipswich tunnel, Stratford and the North London line to the ECML via Canonbury and Finsbury Park or the WCML via Primrose Hill. Port expansion means that it is of the utmost importance that alternative W9 and W10 routes are developed.'

There is a need to accommodate more and longer freight trains.

Infrastructure investment

Network Rail are developing a scheme for the remodelling of Bow Junction that could allow trains from the main line to make use of the Electric Line beyond the Crossrail 1 tunnel portal. This would give four tracks fully usable by passenger trains from Stratford into Liverpool Street, in addition to those which will be in the Crossrail tunnels.

The company are also pursuing the electrification of the Gospel Oak to Barking line. This would allow an electrified diversionary route across London for Thames-side freight as well as providing relief on the Great Eastern between Forest Gate and Stratford. It would also avoid the need for double heading (electric

plus diesel) or locomotive change for freights routed this way.

The two-car dmus could then be replaced by four-car emus, which would in turn permit a homogenised fleet for all London Overground services. It would also open up some more service provision possibilities, such as Clapham Junction to Barking.

It is not feasible to operate additional outer suburban and long distance services over the GEML without a prohibitively expensive capacity upgrade between Shenfield and Liverpool Street. As a long term option, it is therefore proposed to consider four tracking between Colchester and Chelmsford and then building a new link across to the LUL Central Line and then running into the proposed Crossrail 2 (Chelsea-Hackney) alignment, thereby allowing additional outer services to operate.'

It will be recalled that Crossrail 2 is intended to take over the Epping branch of the Central line before entering new construction in the Hackney area. Who knows, the route might even take in Ongar ...?

Maintenance

It should be added that heavy mixed usage of the nature described has its counterpart in growing maintenance and renewals needs, for which time must also be found. The questions are how, and when?

A pattern of cyclical possessions has been agreed for the North London group, comprising of five to six

Above: The new Haggerston station was under construction when this view was taken on 12 December 2009. As can be seen, it could be said to blend in well with the park in the foreground and there seems to be little about it to excite local opposition. But this will not always be the case. John Glover

Above: *The new footbridge at Highbury & Islington, spanning all four surface tracks, on 4 June 2010. Here, East London trains terminate and passengers continuing westwards or originating from there need to change. A second means of crossing between the platforms such as this helps spread the crush of people if such proves to be a problem, and a period of complete line closure was a good time in which to install it.* John Glover

hour possessions every weeknight, for the maximum lengths of line that the overnight freight service will permit. This is on a 12-weekly cycle, grouped into convenient lengths, though this needed to be reviewed on completion of the East London works.

Will this cater sufficiently for freight growth? Options for improvement are being developed with the completion of gauge enhancement work on the North London group (and also the cross-country route to the Midlands and North via Nuneaton). This will greatly enhance the ability to divert trains at nights and/or weekends to improve maintenance opportunities.

The Watford-Euston DC lines appear in the West Coast Route Plan. On the section used in common with the Bakerloo between Harrow & Wealdstone and Queen's Park, shortcomings in the traction power supply are noted. Continuous welded track is to be installed over the entire line to reduce track failures and improve performance levels.

The usage of the DC lines is by local passenger services only; there is no freight.

West and South London

A similar document covers these areas, entitled 'Sussex'. On the main line from London Bridge, the introduction of London Overground has already occurred, but the revitalised Thameslink service is yet to happen.

The West London line is described as experiencing significant problems with overcrowding of passenger services due to growth in commuter numbers and has been supplemented by additional demand from the new stations at Imperial Wharf and the Westfield shopping centre at Shepherd's Bush. Short hop journeys are said to predominate here. Long term, the outlook is for an eight-car railway for Southern services, which in turn requires a platform lengthening programme. Logically, does that means eight-car trains for London Overground too?

There is what is described as 'a complex network of suburban lines throughout south London. This is characterised by multiple connections between the different lines so that most stations have services to both Victoria and London Bridge'. One of the effects of this is that penetrating services from the north of the river are given a wide choice of potential destinations. This accounts for the various destinations of Thameslink services over the years, including towards Kent, what might be achievable from a West London line approach, and the schemes which have been mooted for the East London line extensions.

The West London line is defined as the most significant freight corridor in this group of routes. The primary traffics are aggregates to and from south east terminals and international trains running between the West Coast or Great Western main lines and the Channel Tunnel. It is the most easterly crossing of the Thames for freight on Network Rail and at the southern end Channel Tunnel services are normally routed via Catford and Maidstone East. It will thus have to share a section of line between Factory Junction (Wandsworth Road) and Longhedge Junction (less than a mile) when the London Overground

service on the Clapham Junction extension from Surrey Quays starts.

The line via Redhill is the only alternative to this for W9 gauge freight traffic, though it requires diesel haulage due to the incompatibility of track circuits and power supply on the route with Class 92 traction.

There are perhaps 30 freight trains a day over the West London, in each direction. Passenger traffic is dominated by London Overground, but there is also an hourly Southern service between East Croydon and Milton Keynes Central.

Present problems

These include:
* For suburban services, limited platform capacity at both London Bridge and Victoria.
* The short and normally 2-car formation of the Victoria-Peckham Rye-London Bridge service, which uses the same platform capacity at both terminals as any other train.
* The flat junction at Battersea Park.
* Passenger congestion at several larger stations, including Clapham Junction. Here, it is recommended that this is combined with the platform lengthening programmes and the straightening of Platforms 14-17. This includes those

used by the Southern's West London trains.
* The conflicts at Gloucester Road Junction (outside Croydon) where the lines from both London Bridge and Victoria converge before approaching West Croydon.
* The lack of capacity for turning trains at either West or East Croydon.
* The flat junctions at both ends of the West London line, with very limited locations suitable for holding freight trains. To allow service increases on the Catford loop and South London lines, there is the possibility of constructing freight loops on the West London line.
* The need to stop to raise/lower the pantograph at the voltage changeover point on the West London line which costs around two minutes, and could be more of less solved for passenger trains by moving that point to Shepherd's Bush station where they will stop anyway.
* The inability to operate Class 92s on freights via Redhill, which reduces the routes to the Channel Tunnel to one.
* Route availability and train length restrictions to specific freight terminals.

Unlike the North London services, the limitations are much more focussed on passenger services than freight.

Above: Work at Canonbury is not complete on 29 June 2010, but there is enough for the North London service provision to be restored, even if the new extensions from the East London cannot yet be operated. This is a train from Stratford formed by No 378004. It is using the north side of the formation and one of the two new platforms; the others, to the right, are still barriered off. But service restoration starts bringing in the money again. John Glover

Above: *Dalston Kingsland is in a physically restricted area, which limits its ability to be expanded. Wherever possible, a consideration of possible future needs if the project is outstandingly successful (as all Project Managers hope!) should be taken into account at the planning stage. That is not to say that it needs to be built now, merely that short-term considerations should not effectively rule it out in future. No 378017 is arriving on 12 December 2009. John Glover*

The future scene

Here too passenger demand on inner suburban services is expected to rise at something approaching 1.5% a year, though it may be that overcrowding is suppressing travel volumes at the moment. If so, the growth rate could be that much higher.

The opening of Shepherd's Bush Overground station in 2008 led to high levels of overcrowding on the West London line. This was as a result of the Westfield development, which saw large numbers of shoppers using the train service. The addition of Imperial Wharf a year later had the effect that it became difficult to board some peak services there. Growth here and at the other stations of West Brompton and Kensington Olympia is likely to reflect what is happening elsewhere on the inner services.

The rebuilding work at London Bridge will reduce capacity while the work is in progress, which is translated into peak services being reduced from approximately 30tph to 24tph. Thus the South London line services to Victoria are being withdrawn in December 2012 when the London Overground services from Surrey Quays to Clapham Junction are

introduced; the latter do not serve the Brighton station at London Bridge.

From March 2012, 10-car suburban services from London Bridge operate on the slow lines via Sydenham, for which platform extensions, signalling works and some switch and crossing work were needed. Items such as Driver Only Operation equipment needed to be repositioned. Some use of Selective Door Opening was also anticipated.

The similar 10-car inner suburban programme for trains from Victoria requires extensive platform lengthening works and a power upgrade; this is anticipated for implementation in December 2013. Both these programmes offer a means of increasing carrying capacity by 25%.

More growth?

The 4-car London Overground trains will look a bit lost on platforms made ready for 10-car trains. Consideration was given in the Route Utilisation Strategies for East London trains to be strengthened to 5-car, 6-car or even 8-car, but this was not recommended before 2020. (There are some very

significant problems at some of the original East London stations.) Meanwhile, the split of the peak service on the Sydenham line is seen as 6tph to London Bridge and 8tph, perhaps 10tph, to the East London.

The 10-car programmes for Southern are anticipated as adding a requirement for 74 more vehicles in total, which will of course have to be sourced. The intention is to use Class 377 units displaced from Southern's Coastway services by the arrival of Class 313s from the North London and Watford DC services. That will cater for the first London Bridge phase. The second phase, the Victoria services, was to depend on the return of those Southern Class 377s leased to Thameslink. This, however, now looks likely to be sourced from new build.

A complementary task is to find, adapt or construct stabling and depot facilities to accommodate 10-car rather than 8-car trains.

As part of the Strategic Freight Network, there is provision for the potential development of Tonbridge-Redhill-Balham as an alternative Channel Tunnel route upgrade compatible with Class 92 haulage. This will involve the conversion of existing track circuits on part of the route and a possible

power supply upgrade. That too would allow through freight operation by one electric locomotive to the West Coast Main Line.

On the engineering side, new or improved track maintenance access points are being considered as are new or improved storage areas at selected points. Major junctions may also receive fixed lighting. Investigations are continuing to find ways of minimising service disruption when works are being undertaken and reduce the need for bus replacement services.

With all these projections, and included here are only those which affect London Overground most directly, there is the uncertainty as to how passengers will react to the new facilities. How will yet more forthcoming changes, such as the revamp and extension of Thameslink services, affect the operation?

The most important issue in this area appears to be how to cope with seemingly ever-increasing peak loads as expeditiously as possible. For this, the answer is a combination of more trains, longer trains, perhaps trains with less seating and more standing, plus selected infrastructure works and timetable revisions, to enable the railway to maximise its carrying capacity where it is wanted.

Above: *Here a Class 378 train crosses Middleton Road, Dalston, on 4 June 2010. The road still needs to go into a shallow dip to provide some height clearance, even though that provided is still sub-standard. Road vehicles would get bigger if they were allowed, but what are the prospects for rail? Is it freight, passenger or both that could use the extra space?* John Glover

CHAPTER 20: **CONCLUSIONS**

What has now been created is dependent to a considerable extent on the early engineers. The group of lines which now comprise those over which London Overground operates had very varied beginnings and some parts, like the core of the East London, were never even intended to carry a railway. But that was the first tunnel to be built under a river, successfully, anywhere in the world.

This was later to become the oldest tunnel on the oldest underground system, but this too was later eclipsed. Thus the Underground was running services through the tunnel from 1884 to 2007, when it closed for conversion work to make it part of the National Rail system.

Role of each line

As the East London line of the Underground, it perhaps never really fulfilled much of a role. Carryings were only in the modest category and, although not

forgotten, the element of having become a railway because nobody could think of any other use for it never quite went away. Hopefully it has now found a new role, connected at both the north and south ends and extended to serve a whole new array of clients with a service to (well, nearly to) central London.

What it undoubtedly offers is connections to an east-west Underground network at Whitechapel and Canada Water, and in future to Crossrail. How will the commuters from West Croydon and Crystal Palace take to this alternative offering to the Southern Railway service to London Bridge?

The other railway operations in the portfolio had different purposes. The builders of the North London line, which was equally crucial to the creation of an orbital service for London, had other ideas too. These centred around freight, as has been recounted. The problem here is that the freight, while still coming from the docks, is of a vastly different nature than it was, both in quantity and its movement demands.

Below: An eastbound freight headed by No 66167 passes through Kensal Rise on the morning of 15 April 2010. This was during a busy period and several services were under way in quick succession. John Glover

Sharing track capacity with local passenger services between Stratford, Canonbury, Camden Road, Willesden Junction and Acton is not easy, and it isn't going to get much easier despite all the initiatives presently under way.

This makes the Euston-Watford DC lines look more of an oasis of easy living, where they quietly plough their own furrow in the way that they have been doing since the 1920s. Some smartening up has been done, and they look the better for it.

The Gospel Oak to Barking service remains diesel operated. Though frequency upgrades had long been promised, they were very slow to appear and it just carried on regardless. The use of this line by more freight services puts more pressure on an upgraded passenger operation.

The West London line has in the post war years grown from effectively no public rail passenger services to up to five trains an hour, from two operators. This is a corridor which perhaps was never properly exploited for what it could offer, but traffic growth is undoubtedly there.

The further 2012 extension of the Overground network to Clapham Junction from Surrey Quays was another ambitious plan to try and make the best of the long-standing South London line, which is another which gave the impression of not fulfilling its potential. To remove that service from both the central London terminals it served seems a strange recipe for a successful outcome, but it has not achieved all that it ought to have done.

Vision

What, then, is the vision of the future?

Nobody could deny that Isambard Kingdom Brunel was a man of vision, who had a directness of purpose and clarity of mind which most would envy. He also exploited innovative ideas, and made them work.

If capacity is the main issue, then we may need to separate out the various types of traffic and create a long distance passenger railway (HS1, HS2, HS3 etc), an everyday passenger railway (the present main lines), an urban railway (as with London Overground, London Underground and the Docklands Light Railway) and a freight railway.

Over time, these will need to evolve into physically separate entities.

Some of these railways will have more of a social connotation than others, and these will need continued public support to ensure that their total income, commercial and otherwise, is sufficient to allow them to prosper.

Maybe this will apply to some extent to them all, when wider National or European objectives such as meeting climate change targets or CO_2 emissions are taken into account.

If you plan ahead, you might get where you want. If you don't plan, you are unlikely to achieve all that you otherwise might. How much agreement is there, political or otherwise, on what the railways of the future should be trying to do?

Above: *The use of the same tracks by London Overground and Southern Railway, as here with Platform 5 at New Cross Gate on 28 June 2010, has two compatible operations working together. And, yes, they are both part of National Rail. The train is formed of No 378151.* John Glover

CONCLUSIONS

Above: *The platforms of the East London Line's Whitechapel station are a good example of using existing infrastructure in a new role. A southbound train formed by No 378146 (note the use of Underground rather than National Rail terminology) is arriving on 28 April 2010.* John Glover

Next 20 years

This book has attempted to describe recent events, and some not so recent, and assess how the network might be further developed. The key point that comes across is that both passenger and freight growth are placing impossible pressures on the railway as a whole. There are ways around this as Network Rail demonstrates but, to put it bluntly, it is going to cost more and more to achieve less and less by way of capacity improvements. Unless, of course, more really big schemes like Crossrail 1 and Thameslink are to be funded and built.

None of this can be achieved easily and quickly; a stable background against which future needs can be debated, worked up and perhaps agreed between the political parties would be the ideal.

Where do Transport for London and London Rail stand in all this? The important issue here seems to be how conflicts between local requirements and a national railway can be resolved with the Department for Transport and Network Rail, to mutual advantage. Benefits for the population of London and its economy are by no means the same as for those elsewhere, and this book has hinted at some of the ways in which they might differ.

Table 20.1: TfL railways compared

Year 2009/10	Train or tram km millions	Passenger journeys millions	Traffic revenue millions
London Underground	70.8	1,047	1,809
Docklands Light Railway	4.4	68	74
London Overground	2.3	27	37
London Tramlink	2.5	27	17
Total	**80.0**	**1,169**	**1,737**
Year 2012/13	Train or tram km millions	Passenger journeys millions	Traffic revenue millions
London Underground	76.7	1,100	1,912
Docklands Light Railway	6.0	90	105
London Overground	5.5	72	96
London Tramlink	2.7	28	20
Total	**90.9**	**1,290**	**2,133**

Above: Substantial new works have taken place at Willesden Junction station. This is the new ticket office on 7 May 2008, reached by a new bridge from the Low Level platform and also by a walkway from the exit to the subway, whose steps take the passenger to the High Level platforms. This avoids the need for High Level platform passengers wishing to leave the station to have to use the stairs to descend all the way to Low Level and walk along the platform before climbing all the way back up again. John Glover

Left: There are some locations where making sizeable improvements is very difficult. To some extent, as here at Rotherhithe, it will depend on how much of the existing infrastructure you can afford to knock down (or will be allowed to by others). This view shows the platforms as reopened on 28 April 2010. John Glover

Other rail operations

Finally, it may be of interest to provide some indication of the size of the London Overground operation compared with that of London Underground, the Docklands Light Railway and London Tramlink (Croydon). Three measures are used in Table 20.1, that of production, usage and revenue. They are shown also for two years, 2009/10 and for 2012/13 by which time London Overground becomes fully operational. These are taken from the TfL Business Plan 2009/10-2017/18.

Thus there is substantial growth forecast throughout this sector, with the possible exception of London Tramlink. The Docklands Light Railway is completing conversion from two to three (articulated) cars and was extended to Stratford International in 2011, while the London Underground upgrade has to deal with by far the greatest number of passengers in total. In reality, the expectations shown here for passenger journeys in 2012/13 were exceeded slightly in 2010/11.

Nevertheless, the future use which is expected to be experienced by London Overground is by far the greatest increase in proportional terms. For this, robust and comprehensive development will continue to be necessary.

It is hoped that this book will have given some insight into how this has been and is being achieved.

APPENDIX A:
LONDON OVERGROUND STATIONS

This list shows the stations presently served by London Overground services, and their history. They are divided into three sections and the present (or last) names are used throughout. Stations are listed alphabetically and the electrification system shown is that relevant to the platforms used by London Overground; other systems may be used elsewhere on the same station.

Abbreviations

ET	Essex Thames-side
LM	London Midland
LO	London Overground
LU	London Underground
NR	Network Rail
SE	Southeastern
SN	Southern
SW	South West Trains
DC 3rd	DC third rail operation
DC 4th	DC fourth rail operation

SECTION 1

Stations open on what in 2011 is part of the London Overground network, where LO is the only rail operator

Station	Opened	Operator	Electrification system	Notes
Acton Central	1 August 1853	LO	DC 3rd/AC	
Brondesbury	2 January 1860	LO	AC	
Brondesbury Park	1 June 1908	LO	AC	
Bushey	1 December 1841	LO	DC 3rd	
Caledonian Road & Barnsbury	21 November 1870	LO	AC	
Camden Road	5 December 1870	LO	AC	
Canonbury	1 September 1858	LO	AC	
Carpenders Park	17 November 1952	LO	DC 3rd	Station resited, original 1914
Crouch Hill	21 July 1868	LO	none	
Dalston Junction	27 April 2010	LO	DC 3rd	
Dalston Kingsland	16 May 1983	LO	AC	
Gospel Oak	2 January 1860	LO	AC	
Gospel Oak (Barking line)	5 January 1981	LO	none	New platform opened
Hackney Central	12 May 1980	LO	AC	
Hackney Wick	12 May 1980	LO	AC	
Haggerston	27 April 2010	LO	DC 3rd	
Hampstead Heath	2 January 1860	LO	AC	
Harringay Green Lanes	1 June 1880	LO	none	
Hatch End	8 August 1842	LO	DC 3rd	
Headstone Lane	10 February 1913	LO	DC 3rd	
Homerton	13 May 1985	LO	AC	
Hoxton	27 April 2010	LO	DC 3rd	
Kensal Rise	1 July 1873	LO	AC	
Kentish Town West	5 October 1981	LO	AC	Rebuilt after prolonged closure
Kilburn High Road	December 1851	LO	DC 4th	
Leyton Midland Road	9 July 1894	LO	none	
Leytonstone High Road	9 July 1894	LO	none	
Rotherhithe	7 December 1869	LO	DC 3rd	
Shadwell	10 April 1876	LO	DC 3rd	
Shoreditch High Street	27 April 2010	LO	DC 3rd	
South Acton	1 January 1880	LO	DC 3rd	
South Hampstead	10 July 1922	LO	DC 3rd	
South Tottenham	1 May 1871	LO	AC	Electrification not used by LO
Surrey Quays	7 December 1869	LO	DC 3rd	

Upper Holloway	21 July 1868	LO	none	
Walthamstow Queen's Rd	9 July 1894	LO	none	
Wanstead Park	9 July 1894	LO	none	
Wapping	7 December 1869	LO	DC 3rd	
Watford High Street	1 October 1862	LO	DC 3rd	DC 4th with Croxley link
West Hampstead	1 March 1888	LO	AC	
Willesden Junction HL	1 September 1866	LO	AC	
Woodgrange Park	9 July 1894	LO	AC	Electrification not used by LO

SECTION 2
Stations open on what in 2011 is part of the London Overground network, where other rail operators are also present

Station	Opened	Operator	Electrification system	Notes
Anerley	5 June 1839	LO	DC 3rd	
Barking	13 April 1884	ET	none	
Blackhorse Road	14 December 1981	LU	none	Platforms resited, new entrance
Brockley	6 March 1871	LO	DC 3rd	
Canada Water	19 August 1999	LU	DC 3rd	
Clapham Junction	2 March 1863	SW	DC 3rd	
Crystal Palace	10 June 1854	LO	DC 3rd	
Forest Hill	5 June 1839	LO	DC 3rd	
Gunnersbury	1 January 1869	LU	DC 4th	
Harlesden	15 June 1912	LU	DC 4th	
Harrow & Wealdstone	20 July 1837	LU	DC 4th	
Highbury & Islington	26 September 1850	LU	AC	
Honor Oak Park	1 April 1886	LO	DC 3rd	
Imperial Wharf	29 September 2009	LO	DC 3rd	
Kensal Green	1 October 1916	LU	DC 4th	
Kensington Olympia	2 June 1862	LO	DC 3rd	Public use very variable
Kenton	15 June 1912	LU	DC 4th	
Kew Gardens	1 January 1869	LU	DC 4th	
London Euston	20 July 1837	NR	DC 3rd/AC	AC not used by LO
New Cross	October 1850	SE	DC 3rd	
New Cross Gate	5 June 1839	LO	DC 3rd	
North Wembley	15 June 1912	LU	DC 4th	
Norwood Junction	5 June 1839	LO	DC 3rd	
Penge West	1 July 1863	LO	DC 3rd	
Queen's Park	3 June 1879	LU	DC 4th	
Richmond	27 July 1846	SW	DC 3rd	
Shepherds Bush	29 September 2008	LO	DC 3rd	
South Kenton	3 July 1933	LU	DC 4th	
Stonebridge Park	15 June 1912	LU	DC 4th	
Stratford High Level	24 April 2009	NR	AC	New platforms for LO
Sydenham	5 June 1839	LO	DC 3rd	
Watford Junction	15 June 1912	LM	DC 3rd	Potential for DC 4th
Wembley Central	8 August 1842	LU	DC 4th	
West Brompton (new)	30 May 1999	LU	DC 3rd	
West Croydon	5 June 1839	LO	DC 3rd	
Whitechapel	10 April 1876	LU	DC 3rd	
Willesden Junction LL	15 June 1912	LO	DC 4th	

SECTION 3
Stations not served in 2011 by London Overground, but will be so served when Phase 2 works are completed

Station	Opened	Operator	Electrification system	Notes
Clapham High Street	1 May 1867	SN	DC 3rd	
Denmark Hill (LBSCR)	13 August 1866	SE	DC 3rd	
Peckham Rye (LBSCR)	13 August 1866	SN	DC 3rd	
Queens Road Peckham	13 August 1866	SN	DC 3rd	
Wandsworth Road	1 May 1867	SN	DC 3rd	

Above: *Freight and local passenger operations do not really mix well. Here, Freightliner's No 66623 takes its train eastwards steadily though Highbury & Islington on 29 June 2010, nicely slotted in between London Overground services. But it will not always work like this, and rather different acceleration and braking characteristics, plus the train load, length and the time taken can play havoc with joint operations.* John Glover

SECTION 4

Other stations of relevance, mostly closed. 'Closure' may refer to the platforms concerned, not necessarily the whole station. Where a station was formerly closed and later reopened, this did not necessarily use the same site

Station	Opened	Closed	Notes
Blackhorse Road	9 July 1894	13 December 1981	Platforms resited
Broad Street	1 November 1865	30 June 1986	Site redeveloped
Canning Town	29 October 1995	9 December 2006	Resited, now DLR conversion
Croxley Green	15 June 1912	26 September 2003	Taxi replacement ended
Custom House	26 November 1865	9 December 2006	Crossrail to use site
Dalston Kingsland	9 November 1850	1 November 1865	Replaced by Dalston Junction
Dalston Junction	1 November 1865	30 June 1986	New station 2010
Haggerston	2 September 1867	6 May 1940	New station 2010
Homerton	1 October 1868	23 April 1945	New station 2010
Kentish Town West	1 April 1867	18 April 1971	Closed by fire damage
North Woolwich	14 June 1847	9 December 2006	Abandoned
Primrose Hill	5 May 1855	22 September 1992	Abandoned but still in situ
Rickmansworth Church St	1 October 1862	3 March 1952	Abandoned
Shoreditch (EL)	10 April 1876	9 June 2006	Abandoned
Shoreditch (NLL)	1 November 1865	4 October 1940	Bomb damage
Silvertown	19 June 1863	9 December 2006	Abandoned
Stratford Low Level	16 October 1854	9 December 2006	DLR conversion
Watford Stadium	4 December 1982	14 May 1993	Private station, football only
Watford West	15 June 1912	26 September 2003	Taxi replacement ended
West Brompton	1 September 1866	21 October 1940	New station 1999
West Ham	14 May 1979	9 December 2006	DLR conversion

Note that many stations, particularly those on the East London Line but also Kensington Olympia, did not have a continuous service over the whole period shown.

The East London Line was not served by any part of what became London Underground (as opposed to the main-line railway companies) before 1884. It was electrified in 1913, and the line as a whole was vested in London Transport at nationalisation in 1948. It was transferred to London Overground following the cessation of London Underground operation at the close of 2007.

APPENDIX B:
INTER-STATION DISTANCES

These are all recorded in miles and chains, as used on the national railway network. 1 chain is 22 yards, and there are 80 chains to the mile.

The journey times are those of the first train after 11:00, Mondays to Fridays, in the direction shown for the timetable dated 23 May 2010 to 11 December 2010. All trains stop at all intermediate stations.

Section 1: London Euston to Watford Junction, DC lines

Section	Distance	Cumulative
London Euston-South Hampstead	2m 33ch	2m 33ch
South Hampstead-Kilburn High Road	0m 48ch	3m 01ch
Kilburn High Road-Queen's Park	0m 54ch	3m 55ch
Queen's Park-Kensal Green	0m 66ch	4m 41ch
Kensal Green-Willesden Junction LL	0m 75ch	5m 36ch
Willesden Junction LL-Harlesden	0m 52ch	6m 08ch
Harlesden-Stonebridge Park	0m 76ch	7m 04ch
Stonebridge Park-Wembley Central	1m 05ch	8m 09ch
Wembley Central-North Wembley	0m 60ch	8m 69ch
North Wembley-South Kenton	0m 56ch	9m 35ch
South Kenton-Kenton	0m 69ch	10m 24ch
Kenton-Harrow & Wealdstone	1m 06ch	11m 30ch
Harrow & Wealdstone-Headstone Lane	1m 15ch	12m 45ch
Headstone Lane-Hatch End	0m 60ch	13m 25ch
Hatch End-Carpenders Park	1m 32ch	14m 57ch
Carpenders Park-Bushey	1m 27ch	16m 04ch
Bushey-Watford High Street	0m 63ch	16m 67ch
Watford High Street-Watford Junction	0m 69ch	17m 56ch

Total stations	19
Average inter-station distance	0m 79ch
Off-peak time, end-to-end journey	47 minutes
Average speed, end-to-end journey	22.6mph

Section 2: Richmond to Stratford via Hampstead Heath

Section	Distance	Cumulative
Richmond-Kew Gardens	1m 29ch	1m 29ch
Kew Gardens-Gunnersbury	1m 05ch	2m 34ch
Gunnersbury-South Acton	0m 44ch	2m 78ch
South Acton-Acton Central	0m 59ch	3m 57ch
Acton Central-Willesden Junction HL	1m 79ch	5m 56ch
Willesden Junction HL-Kensal Rise	0m 78ch	6m 54ch
Kensal Rise-Brondesbury Park	0m 50ch	7m 24ch
Brondesbury Park-Brondesbury	0m 35ch	7m 58ch
Brondesbury-West Hampstead	0m 41ch	8m 19ch
West Hampstead-Finchley Road & Frognal	0m 39ch	8m 58ch
Finchley Road & Frognal-Hampstead Heath	0m 63ch	9m 41ch
Hampstead Heath-Gospel Oak	0m 47ch	10m 08ch
Gospel Oak-Kentish Town West	0m 52ch	10m 60ch
Kentish Town West-Camden Road	0m 43ch	11m 23ch
Camden Road-Caledonian Road & Barnsbury	1m 07ch	12m 30ch
Caledonian Road & Barnsbury-Highbury & Islington	0m 38ch	12m 68ch
Highbury & Islington-Canonbury	0m 43ch	13m 31ch
Canonbury-Dalston Kingsland	0m 67ch	14m 18ch
Dalston Kingsland-Hackney Central	0m 72ch	15m 12ch
Hackney Central-Homerton	0m 49ch	15m 61ch
Homerton-Hackney Wick	0m 67ch	16m 48ch
Hackney Wick-Stratford	1m 02ch	17m 50ch

Total stations	23
Average inter-station distance	0m 64ch
Off-peak time, end-to-end journey	63 minutes
Average speed, end-to-end journey	16.8mph

Section 3: West London Line

Section	Distance	Cumulative
Clapham Junction-Imperial Wharf	1m 50ch	1m 50ch
Imperial Wharf-West Brompton	0m 73ch	2m 43ch
West Brompton-Kensington (Olympia)	0m 79ch	3m 42ch
Kensington (Olympia)-Shepherds Bush	0m 53ch	4m 15ch
Shepherds Bush-Willesden Junction HL	2m 20ch	6m 35ch

Total stations	6
Average inter-station distance	1m 23ch
Off-peak time, end-to-end journey	22 minutes
Average speed, end-to-end journey	17.6mph

Left: *Stratford has a long association with the railway industry, and the London Borough of Newham decided to display this locomotive (which it owns) on a plinth outside Stratford Regional station in 1999. Robert is an Avonside 0-6-0ST built in Bristol in 1933 for the Staveley Iron & Chemical Co Ltd for use at its Lamport ironstone quarries in Northamptonshire. It was withdrawn in 1969. Vaguely similar locomotives were employed at the local Beckton Gas Works, the largest producer of town gas in Europe. Robert is now re-exhibited, and was given a new coat of 'Colchester Crimson' paint by the Olympic Delivery Authority. This photograph was taken at Stratford in 2001. John Glover*

INTER-STATION DISTANCES

Section 4: Gospel Oak to Barking

Section	Distance	Cumulative
Gospel Oak-Upper Holloway	1m 16ch	1m 16ch
Upper Holloway-Crouch Hill	0m 65ch	2m 01ch
Crouch Hill-Harringay Green Lanes	0m 76ch	2m 77ch
Harringay Green Lanes-South Tottenham	1m 08ch	4m 05ch
South Tottenham-Blackhorse Road	1m 32ch	5m 37ch
Blackhorse Road-Walthamstow Queen's Road	0m 70ch	6m 27ch
Walthamstow Queen's Road-Leyton Midland Road	1m 11ch	7m 38ch
Leyton Midland Road-Leytonstone High Road	0m 58ch	8m 16ch
Leytonstone High Road-Wanstead Park	1m 15ch	9m 31ch
Wanstead Park-Woodgrange Park	0m 70ch	10m 21ch
Woodgrange Park-Barking	1m 57ch	11m 78ch

Total stations	12
Average inter-station distance	1m 07ch
Off-peal time, end-to-end journey	36 minutes
Average speed, end-to-end journey	20.0mph

Section 5: Dalston Junction to West Croydon

Section	Distance	Cumulative
Dalston Junction-Haggerston	0m 32ch	0m 32ch
Haggerston-Hoxton	0m 41ch	0m 73ch
Hoxton-Shoreditch High Street	0m 58ch	1m 51ch
Shoreditch High Street-Whitechapel	0m 58ch	2m 29ch
Whitechapel-Shadwell	0m 49ch	2m 78ch
Shadwell-Wapping	0m 39ch	3m 37ch
Wapping-Rotherhithe	0m 26ch	3m 63ch
Rotherhithe-Canada Water	0m 17ch	4m 00ch
Canada Water-Surrey Quays	0m 26ch	4m 26ch

Section	Distance	Cumulative
Surrey Quays-New Cross Gate	1m 21ch	5m 47ch
New Cross Gate-Brockley	0m 66ch	6m 33ch
Brockley-Honor Oak Park	1m 03ch	7m 36ch
Honor Oak Park-Forest Hill	0m 71ch	8m 27ch
Forest Hill-Sydenham	0m 62ch	9m 09ch
Sydenham-Penge West	0m 63ch	9m 72ch
Penge West-Anerley	0m 32ch	10m 24ch
Anerley-Norwood Junction	1m 08ch	11m 32ch
Norwood Junction-West Croydon	1m 60ch	13m 12ch

Total stations	19
Average inter-station distance	0m 58ch
Off-peak time, end-to-end journey	51 minutes
Average speed, end-to-end journey	15.5mph

Section 6: Other routes

Section	Distance
Surrey Quays-New Cross	1m 32ch
Sydenham-Crystal Palace	1m 20ch

Section	Distance	Cumulative
Surrey Quays-Queens Road Peckham (est)	1m 34ch	1m 34ch
Queens Road Peckham-Peckham Rye	0m 58ch	2m 12ch
Peckham Rye-Denmark Hill	0m 67ch	2m 79ch
Denmark Hill-Clapham High Street	1m 78ch	4m 77ch
Clapham High Street-Wandsworth Road	0m 31ch	5m 28ch
Wandsworth Road-Clapham Junction	1m 65ch	7m 13ch

Total stations	7
Average inter-station distance	1m 02ch

Source: TRACKmaps publications and similar.

Right: *No 313105 leaves Hampstead Heath on 12 September 2009 with a train for Stratford. It is not too difficult to imagine that there was once much more in the way of canopies and other embellishments at this station, which was extensively rebuilt by British Railways following war damage.* John Glover

BIBLIOGRAPHY AND ACKNOWLEDGEMENTS

Allen, Cecil J. 'Olympia and the West London Line', *Railway World*, August 1969

Borley, H.V. and Kidner, R.W. *The West London Railway and the WLER* (The Oakwood Press, 1981)

Clayton, R., General Editor *The Geography of Greater London* (George Philip & Son Ltd, London, 1964)

Dendy Marshall, C. F., revised by R.W. Kidner *History of the Southern Railway Vol 2* (Ian Allan, 1963)

Frew, Ian (ed) *Britain's Electric Railways Today* (Electric Railway Society, Southern Electric Group, 1983)

Green, C. E.W. (Managing Director Network SouthEast) 'Asset Management' (Conference on Railway Engineering, Adelaide, September 1991)

Hamilton Ellis, C. *British Railway History* (George Allen & Unwin, Vol 1 1954, Vol 2 1959)

Hardy, Brian, Frew, I. D. O. and Wilson, Ross *A Chronology of the Electric Railways of Great Britain and Ireland* (Electric Railway Society monograph, 1981)

Horne, Mike *The Bakerloo Line: An Illustrated History* (Capital Transport Publishing, 2001; ISBN 185414 24 8)

Howard Turner, J.T. *The London, Brighton & South Coast Railway 1: Origins and Development* (Batsford, 1977; ISBN 0 7134 0275 X)

Jacobs, Gerald (ed) *Railway Track Diagrams 2: Eastern* (TRACKmaps 3rd edition, 2006; ISBN 0 9549866 2 0) *Railway Track Diagrams 4: Midlands & North West* (TRACKmaps 2nd edition, 2005; ISBN 0 9549866 0 1) *Railway Track Diagrams 5: Southern & TfL* (TRACKmaps 3rd edition, 2008; ISBN 978 0 9549866 4 3)

James, Leslie *A Chronology of the Construction of Britain's Railways 1778-1855* (Ian Allan Ltd, 1983; ISBN 0 7110 1277 6)

Klapper, C. F. *Sir Herbert Walker's Southern Railway* (Ian Allan, 1973; ISBN 0 7110 0478 1)

Linecar, Howard W.A. *British Electric Trains* (Ian Allan Ltd, London, 1947)

London Rail Study, Part 2 (The Barran Report) (Greater London Council/Department of the Environment, 1974; ISBN 7168 0648 7)

Moving Ahead: Planning Tomorrow's Railways. Route Plan B, Sussex; Route Plan D, East Anglia; Route Plan E, North London Line; Route Plan N, West Coast (Network Rail, all 2010)

Quick, M. E. *Railway Passenger Stations in England, Scotland and Wales: A Chronology* (Third edition, Railway & Canal Historical Society, 2005)

A Rail Strategy for London's Future: Statement of Case (Transport for London, 2007.)

Reed, M. C. *London & North Western Railway* (Atlantic Transport Publishers, 1996; ISBN 0 906899 66 4)

Rose, Douglas, *The London Underground: A Diagrammatic History* (Eighth edition, December 2007)

Vickers, R. L. *DC Electric Trains and Locomotives in the British Isles* (David & Charles, Newton Abbot, 1986; ISBN 0 7153 8674 3)

White, H. P. *A Regional History of the Railways of Great Britain, Vol 3* Greater London (Phoenix House, London, 1963)

Network Rail, London Rail
Various issues of *The Railway Magazine, Railways/Railway World, Trains Illustrated/Modern Railways*. Particular thanks are expressed to *The Railway Magazine,* for permission to use various historical maps that have appeared in that publication in the past.

In compiling this book, I have drawn upon many discussions with and attended lectures by those throughout the industry but particularly those in London Rail, Network Rail and London Travelwatch. I have not mentioned names, as what you read is an amalgam of all of these, but I would like to express my gratitude to everybody concerned. The views expressed are my own, other than where specific sources are given.

INDEX